198 *Easy* WOOD PROJECTS

By
Floyd Morris

SOUTH HOLLAND, ILLINOIS

THE GOODHEART-WILLCOX CO., Inc.

Publishers

Copyright 1970

By

THE GOODHEART-WILLCOX CO., INC.

No part of this book may be reproduced in any form without violating the copyright law. Printed in U. S. A. Library of Congress Catalog Card No. 78-111282.
Standard Book Number 87006-111-9.

56789-70

MAKING PROJECTS FROM THESE PATTERNS

(Note: All dimensions are in inches)

Many project patterns are full size. These may be cut from the plan sheets and pasted onto the stock, using rubber cement; traced onto the stock using carbon paper and pencil; or, traced onto transparent paper and rubber cemented to the stock. After completing a tracing job, it is well to go over lines which should be straight, using a ruler and pencil. Pencil marks not removed by sawing may be removed with an eraser, if not too deep.

To enlarge squared patterns and designs, number outside squares of pattern vertically and horizontally. Lay out squares size indicated, on large sheet of paper. Number squares, then sketch design from small squares into larger squares freehand. Use French curve and ruler to even up lines.

Either Power Or Hand-Operated Saw May Be Used

In making these projects sawing may be done, using either a power-operated jig saw, or a hand-operated scroll saw which has a frame of sufficient depth to permit sawing to the center of the design.

When using a power saw, be sure to use a blade that leaves the edges smooth and to operate the saw so the blade runs in a true vertical position. Follow the lines carefully. Steady even pressure on the stock should be maintained when feeding it into the saw. In making curved cuts care must be taken not to push the stock sideways, and not to make curved cuts short enough to cause burning of the wood or twisting of the blade.

Making an internal cutout without making an entering cut is done by first drilling a hole large enough to take the saw blade through the waste stock which is to be sawed out, raising the hold-down guide on the saw as high as it will go, and placing the hole in the stock over the protruding saw blade. The blade is then refastened at the top and the guide adjusted.

Sanding

After sawing, use medium and fine grit abrasive paper (garnet paper is good) to smooth the edges and rough spots, and correct minor inaccuracies in sawing.

Wood Finishing

Paint Finish: A good even coat of paint or enamel may be obtained if coat of thin shellac (spar varnish for exterior projects) precedes the application of paint. Let this dry well before applying paint or enamel of your choice. Finishes which come in aerosol cans are ideal for small jobs.

Varnish and Penetrating Finishes: Numerous finishes are available. Application procedures vary. Be sure to follow the manufacturer's directions.

Do A Good Job

In making up projects described in this book, take your time and do good work on each and every operation. Take particular care to do a good job on painting and wood finishing. Keep in mind the fact that much of the success of these projects depends on the quality of the finish job.

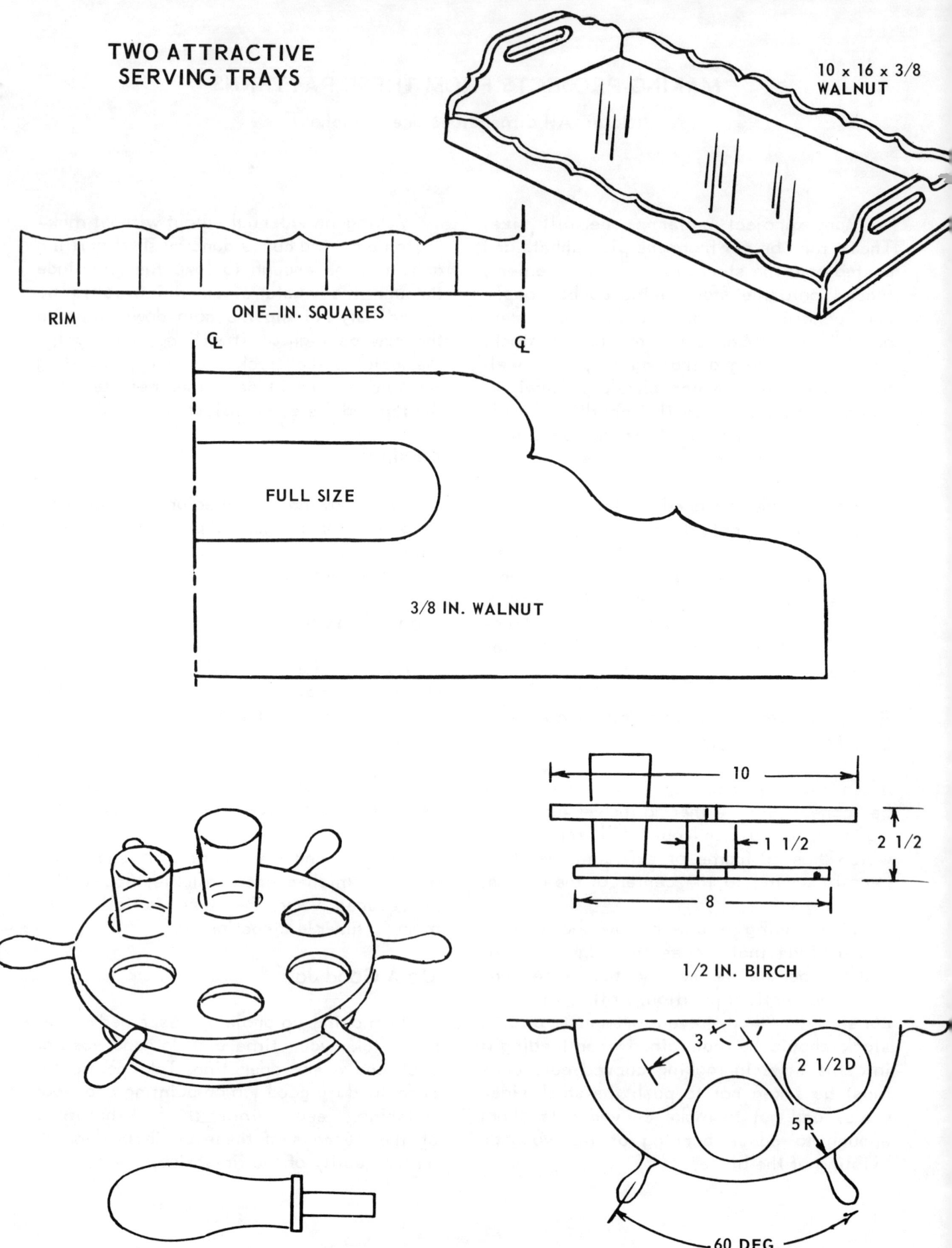

TWO ATTRACTIVE SERVING TRAYS

10 x 16 x 3/8 WALNUT

RIM — ONE-IN. SQUARES

FULL SIZE

3/8 IN. WALNUT

1/2 IN. BIRCH

FULL SIZE

60 DEG.

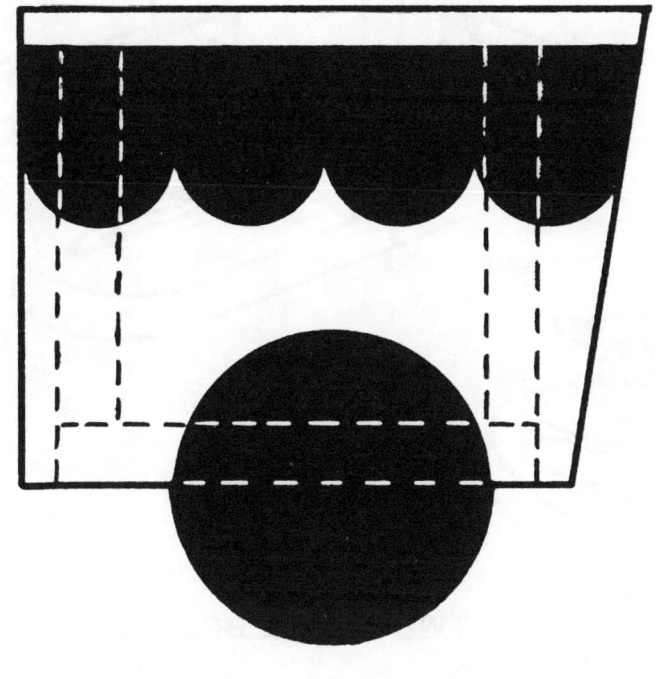

DOGGIE AND CART TO "HAUL" POTTED PLANTS

In making this little planter, 3/8 in. solid stock is suggested for all parts except the doggie cutout; for this part 1/4 in. is better. Give wood two coats of spar varnish; paint on trim – black for dog and red for cart.

FULL SIZE

BOTTOM

END (2 REQD.)

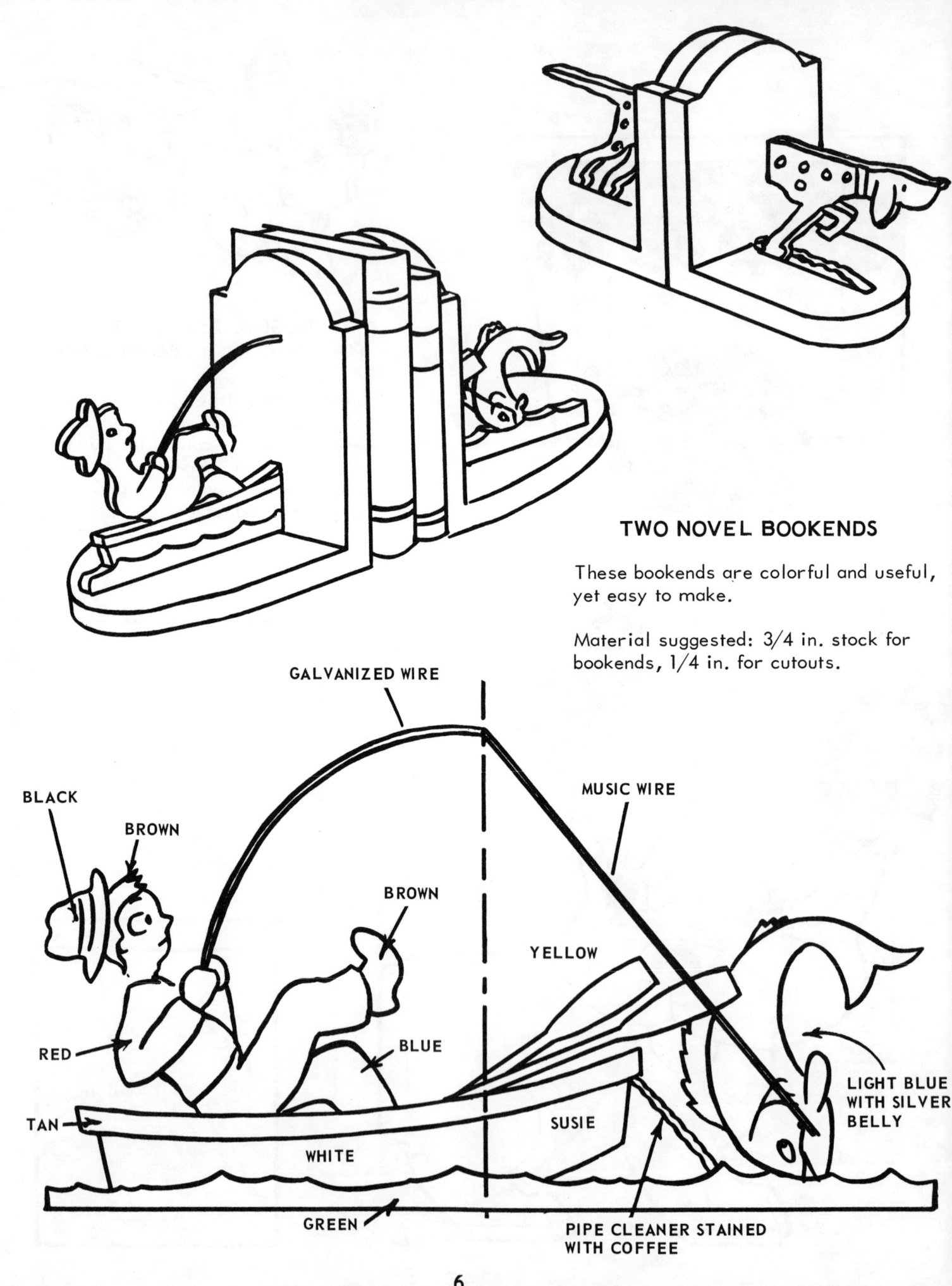

TWO NOVEL BOOKENDS

These bookends are colorful and useful, yet easy to make.

Material suggested: 3/4 in. stock for bookends, 1/4 in. for cutouts.

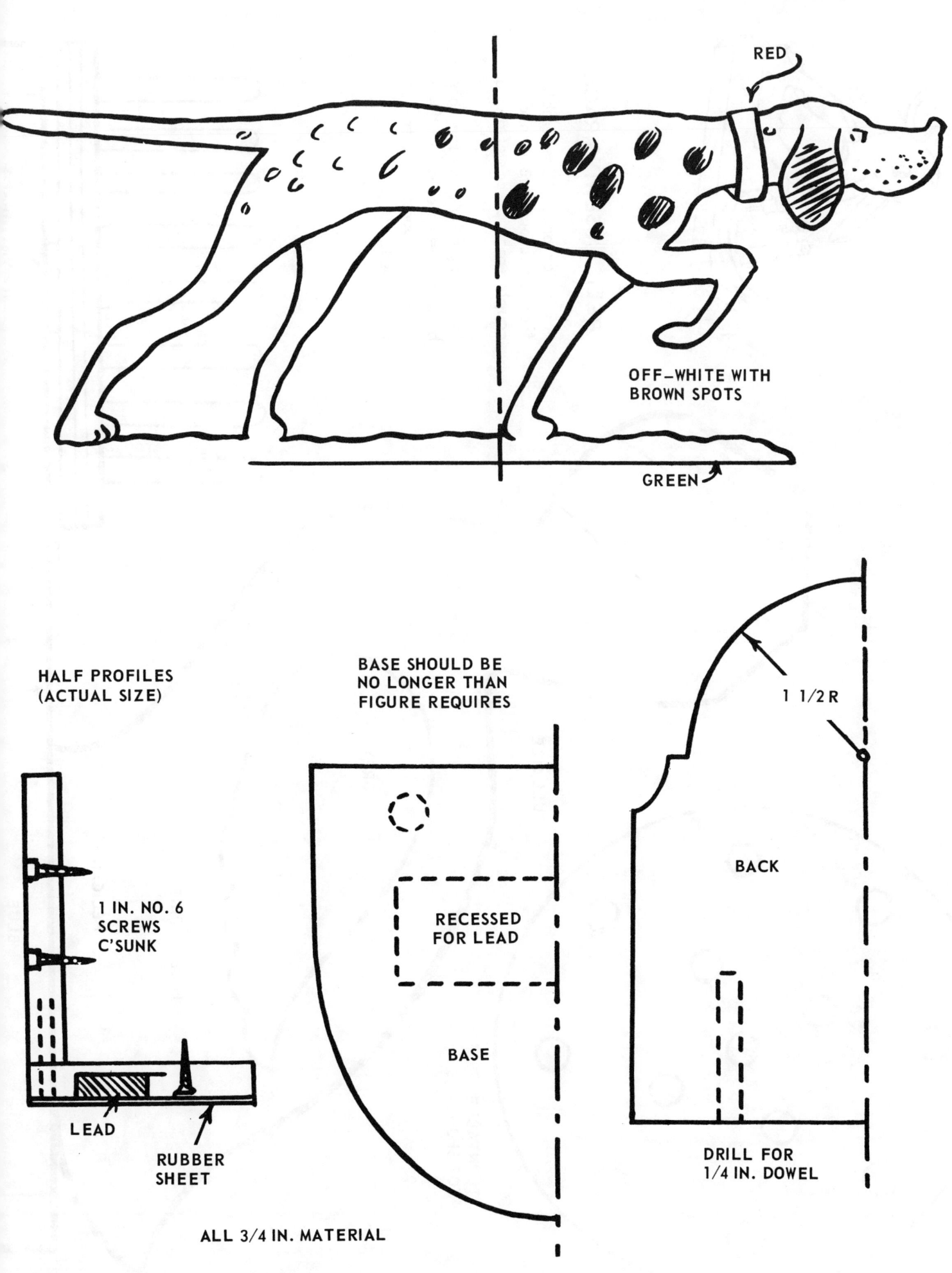

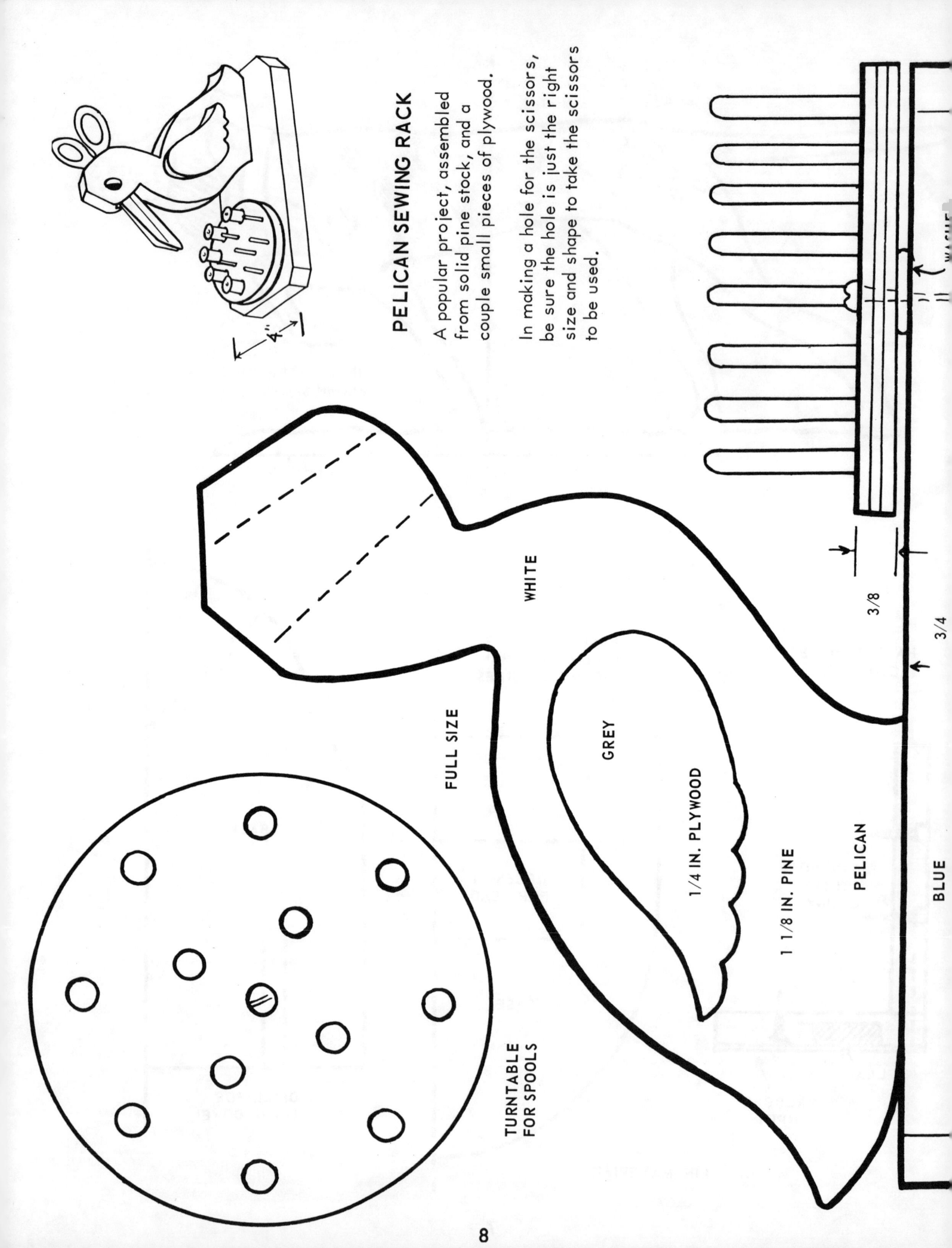

PERSONALIZED HOUSE MARKER

A marker with your address, and a silhouette of your pet, will make a distinctive addition to your home. It's easy to make too, using the full size patterns which are furnished.

The drawing at the left shows how the marker looks when finished.

PROCEDURE: Trace design and numbers to be used onto transparent paper. Fasten pattern to 1/8 or 1/4 in. outdoor plywood, or hardboard, using rubber cement.

Cut out with power or hand-operated saw.

Sand edges, then apply finish of flat black, or white paint. Use a nail or a screw to fasten marker in place on house, or porch.

1234567890

DRAWER HANDLES

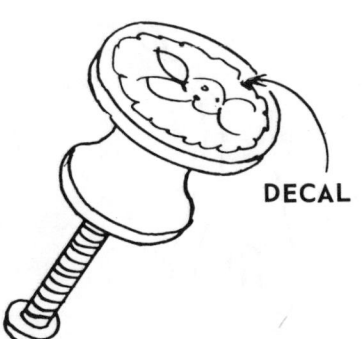
DECAL

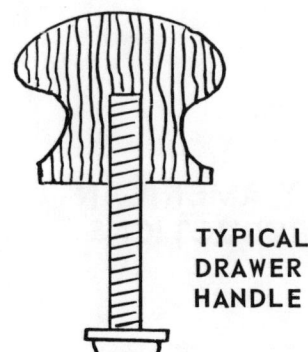
TYPICAL DRAWER HANDLE

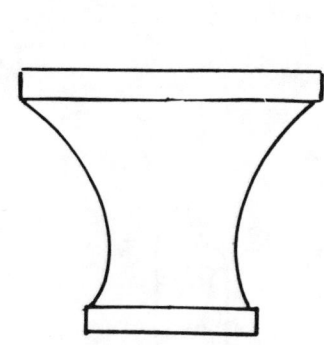

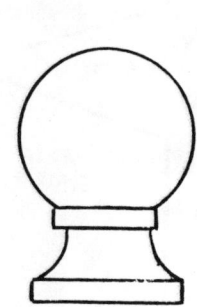 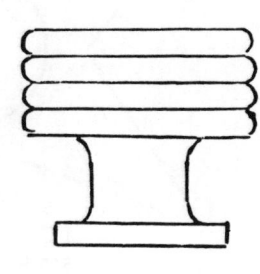 

ALL FULL SIZE HARDWOOD

NUMERAL PATTERNS

For use in making personalized house markers, house numbers, etc.

GRAIN SCOOP PLANTER

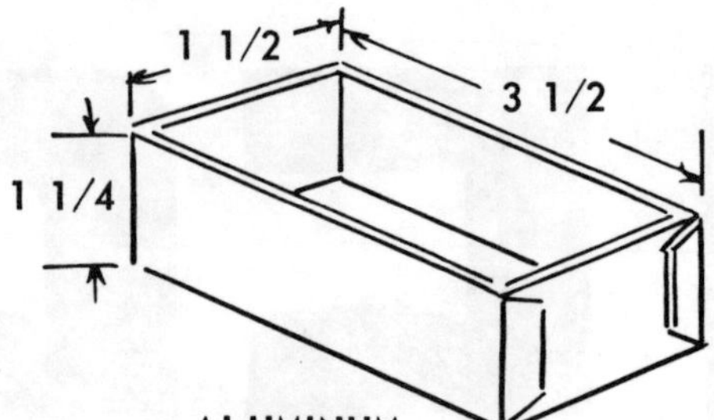

ALUMINUM TANK 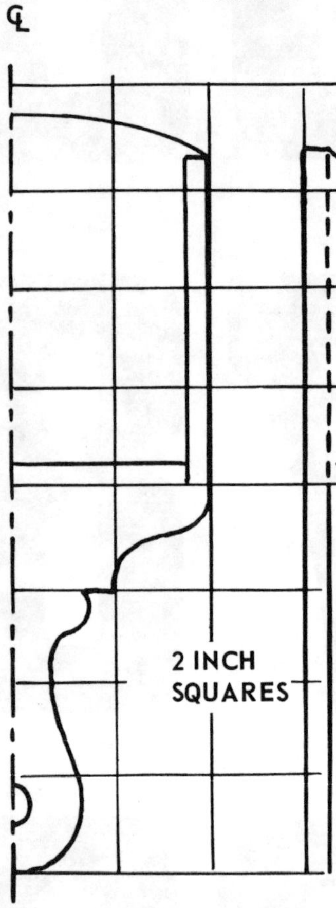 — 1 1/2, 3 1/2, 1 1/4

1/4 IN. PINE

2 INCH SQUARES

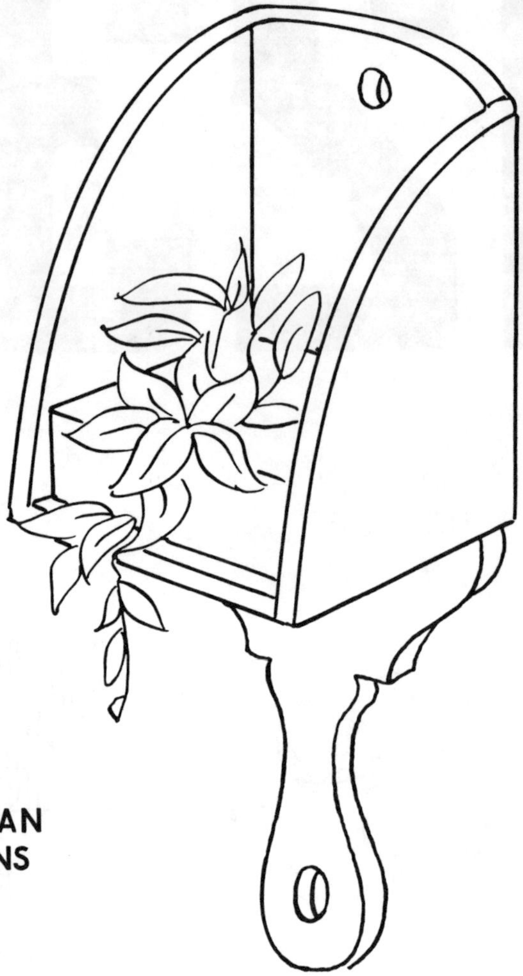

EARLY AMERICAN REPRODUCTIONS

STAR CANDLE HOLDER

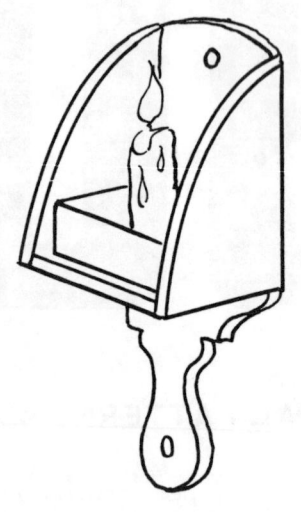

CANDLE HOLDER

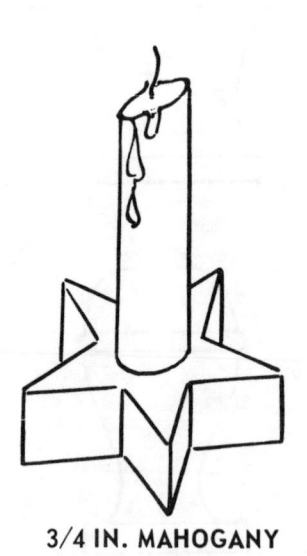

3/4 IN. MAHOGANY

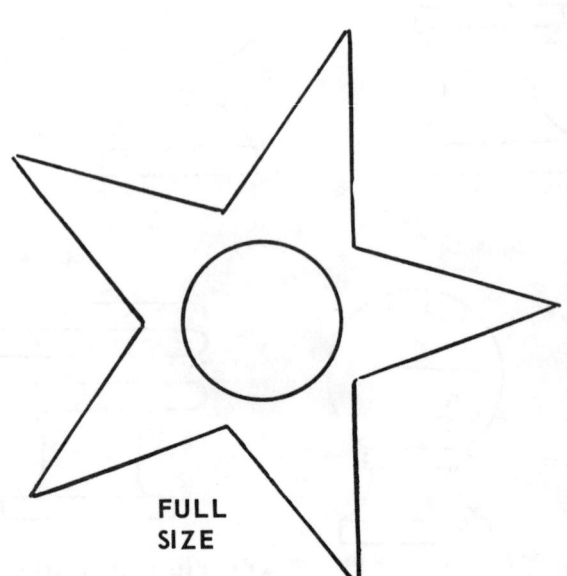

FULL SIZE

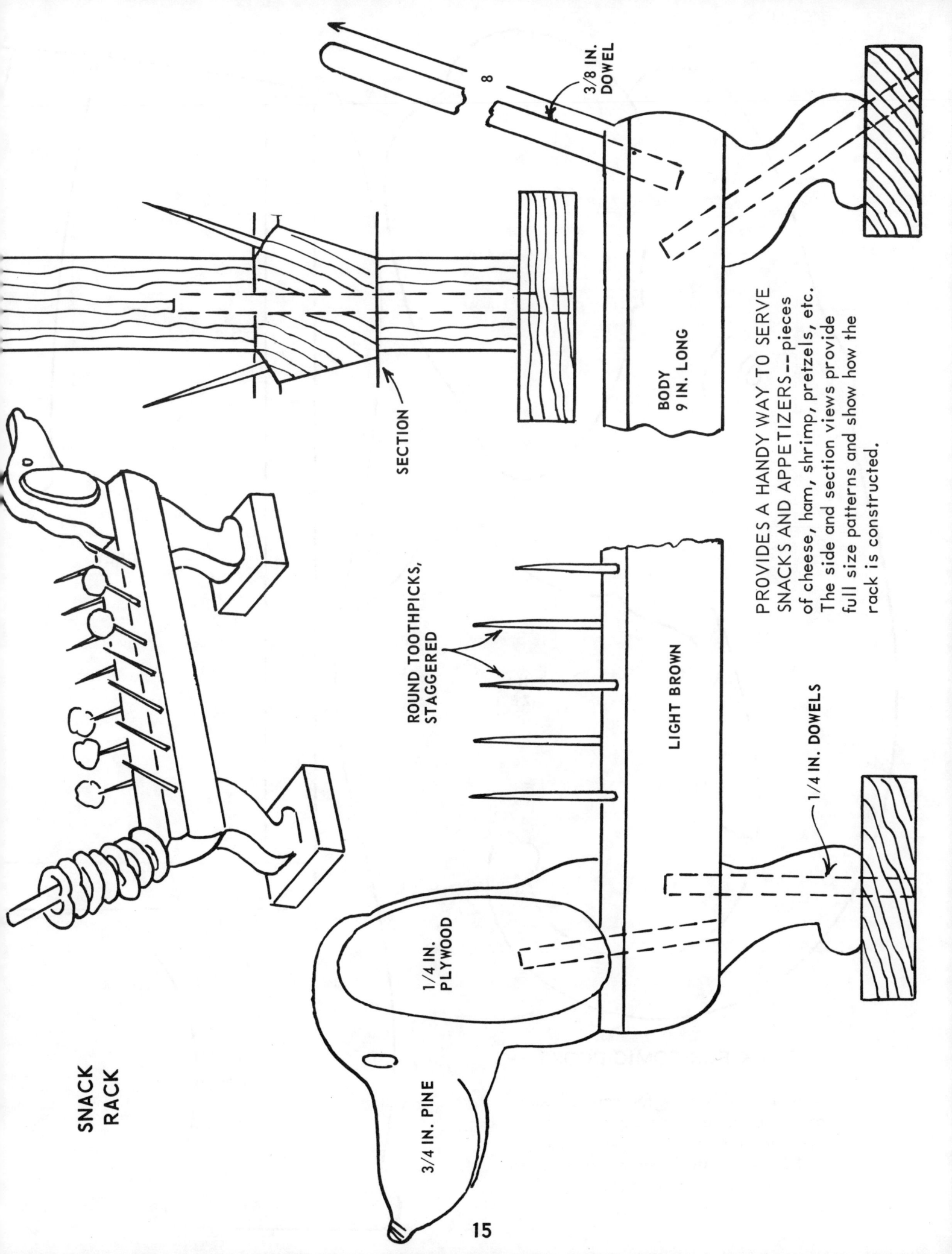

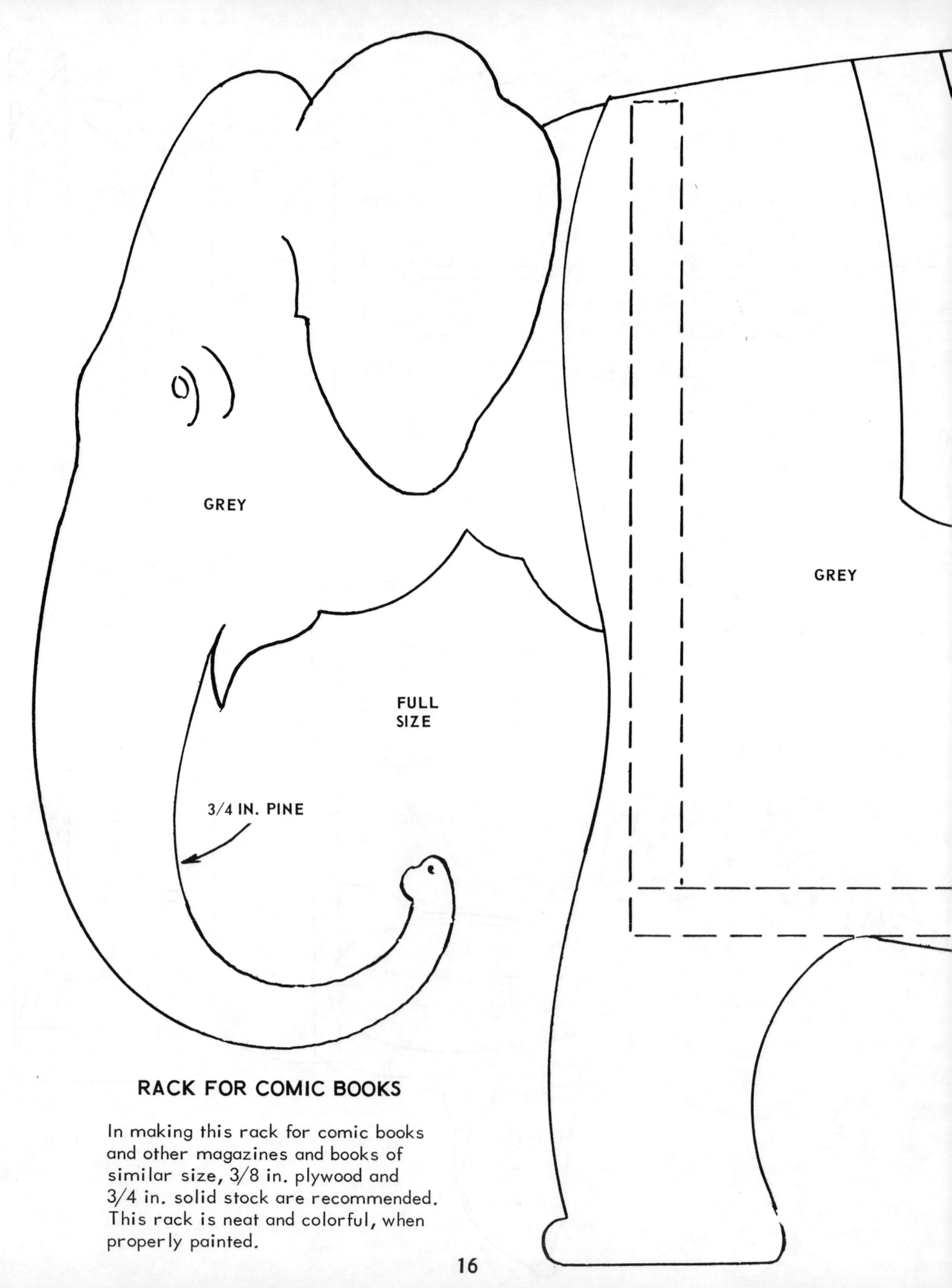

GREY

FULL SIZE

3/4 IN. PINE

GREY

RACK FOR COMIC BOOKS

In making this rack for comic books and other magazines and books of similar size, 3/8 in. plywood and 3/4 in. solid stock are recommended. This rack is neat and colorful, when properly painted.

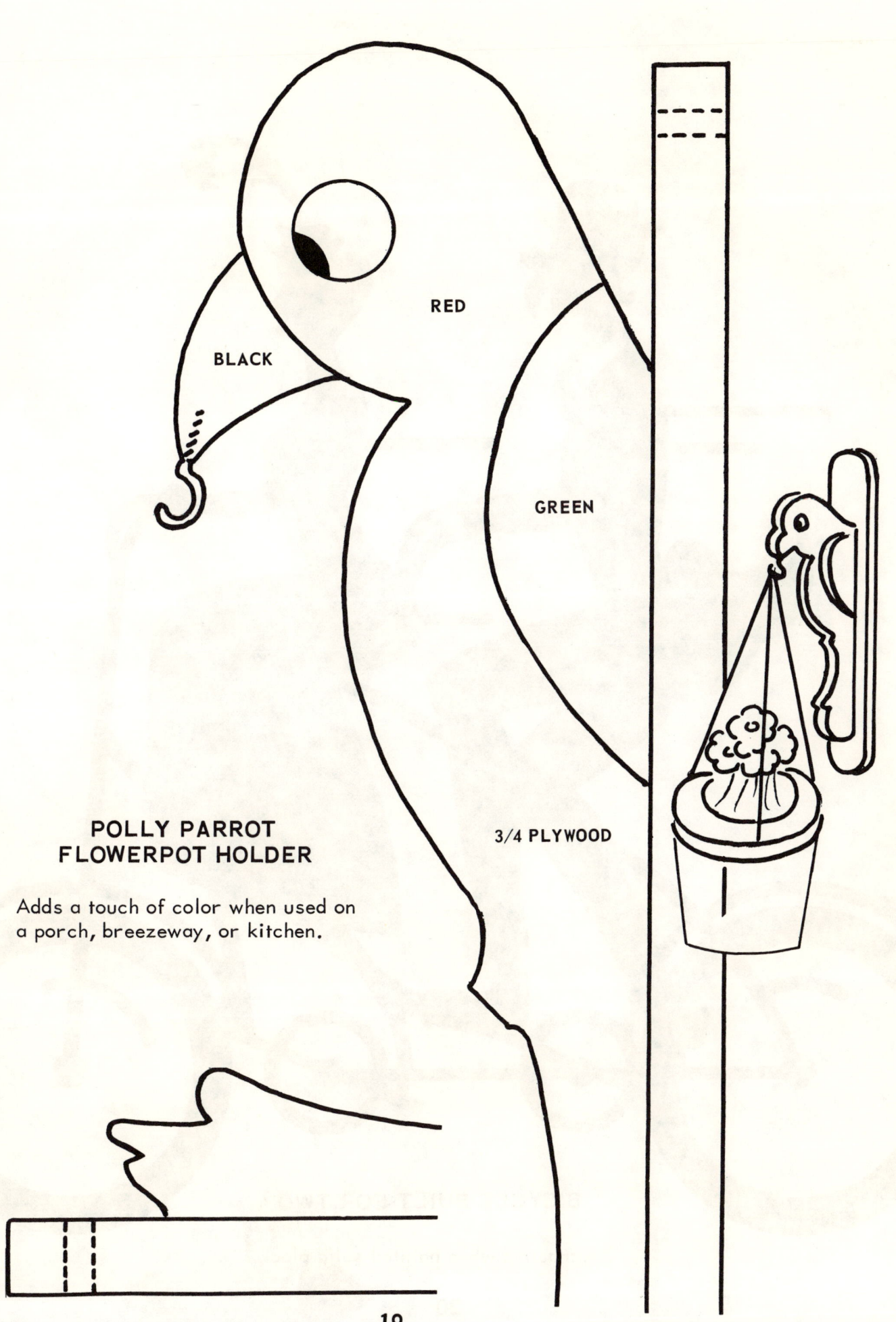

POLLY PARROT FLOWERPOT HOLDER

Adds a touch of color when used on a porch, breezeway, or kitchen.

BICYCLE BUILT FOR TWO

Attractive when painted solid black.

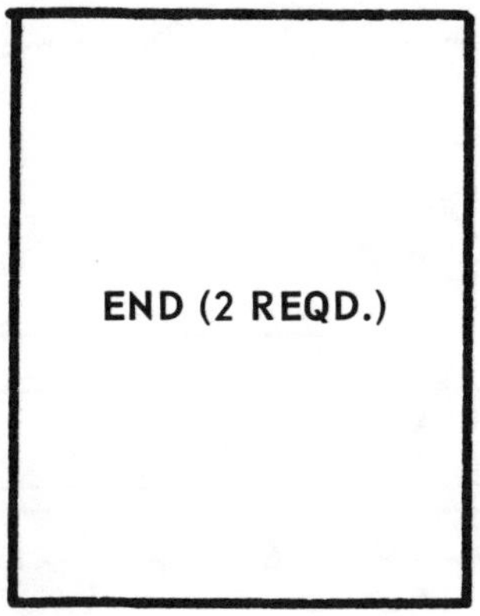

END (2 REQD.)

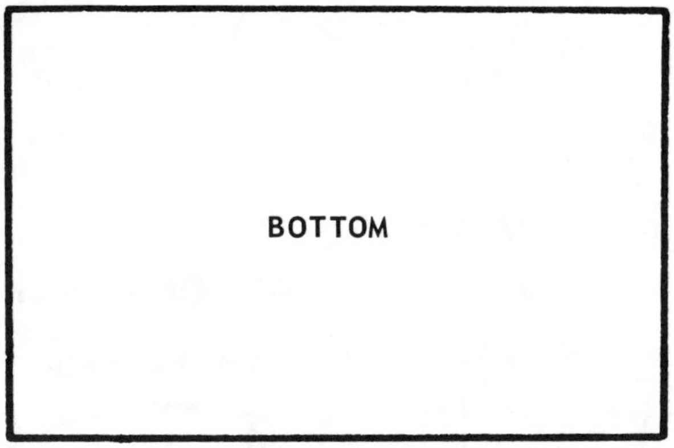

BOTTOM

DOGGY PLANTER

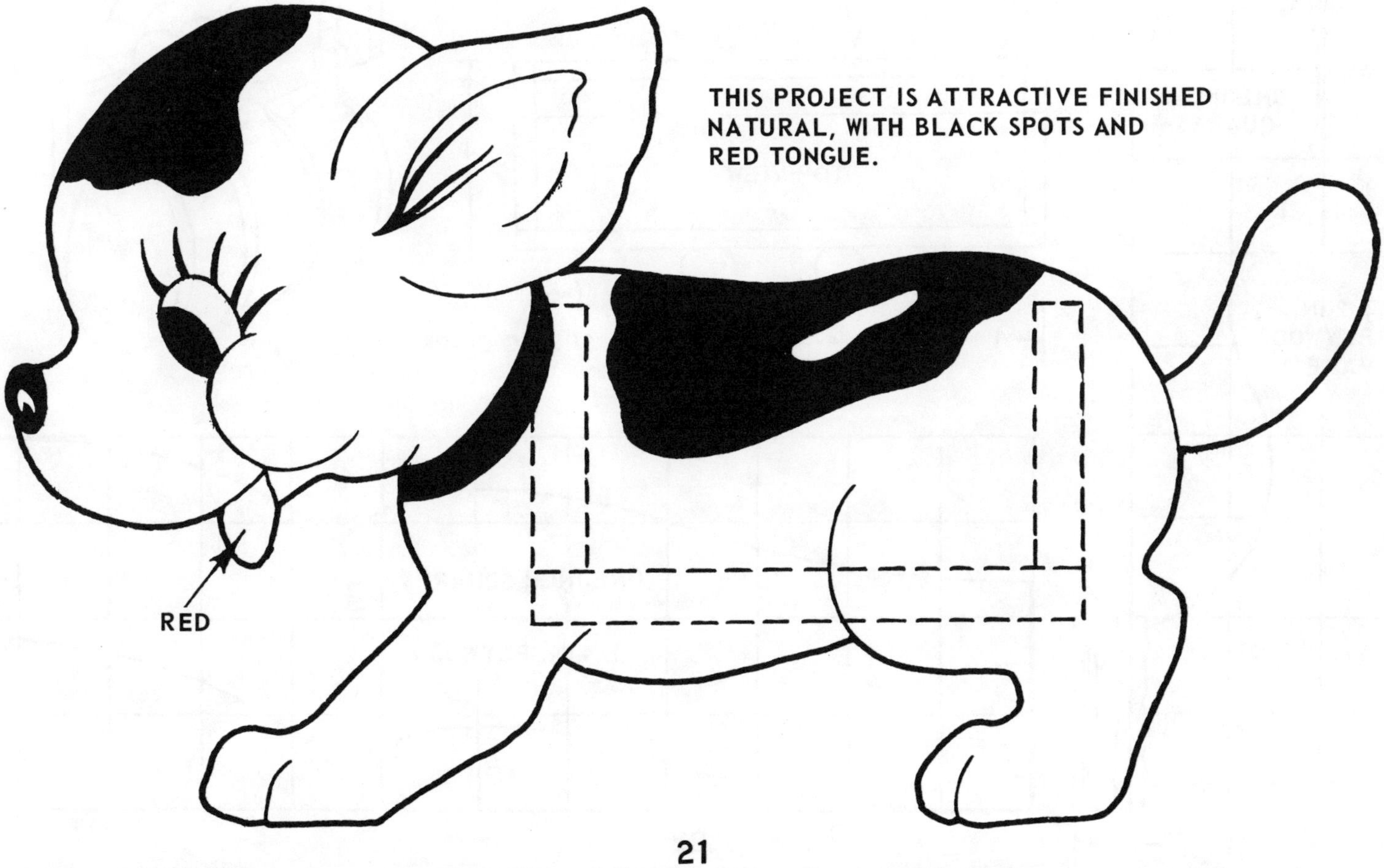

THIS PROJECT IS ATTRACTIVE FINISHED NATURAL, WITH BLACK SPOTS AND RED TONGUE.

RED

21

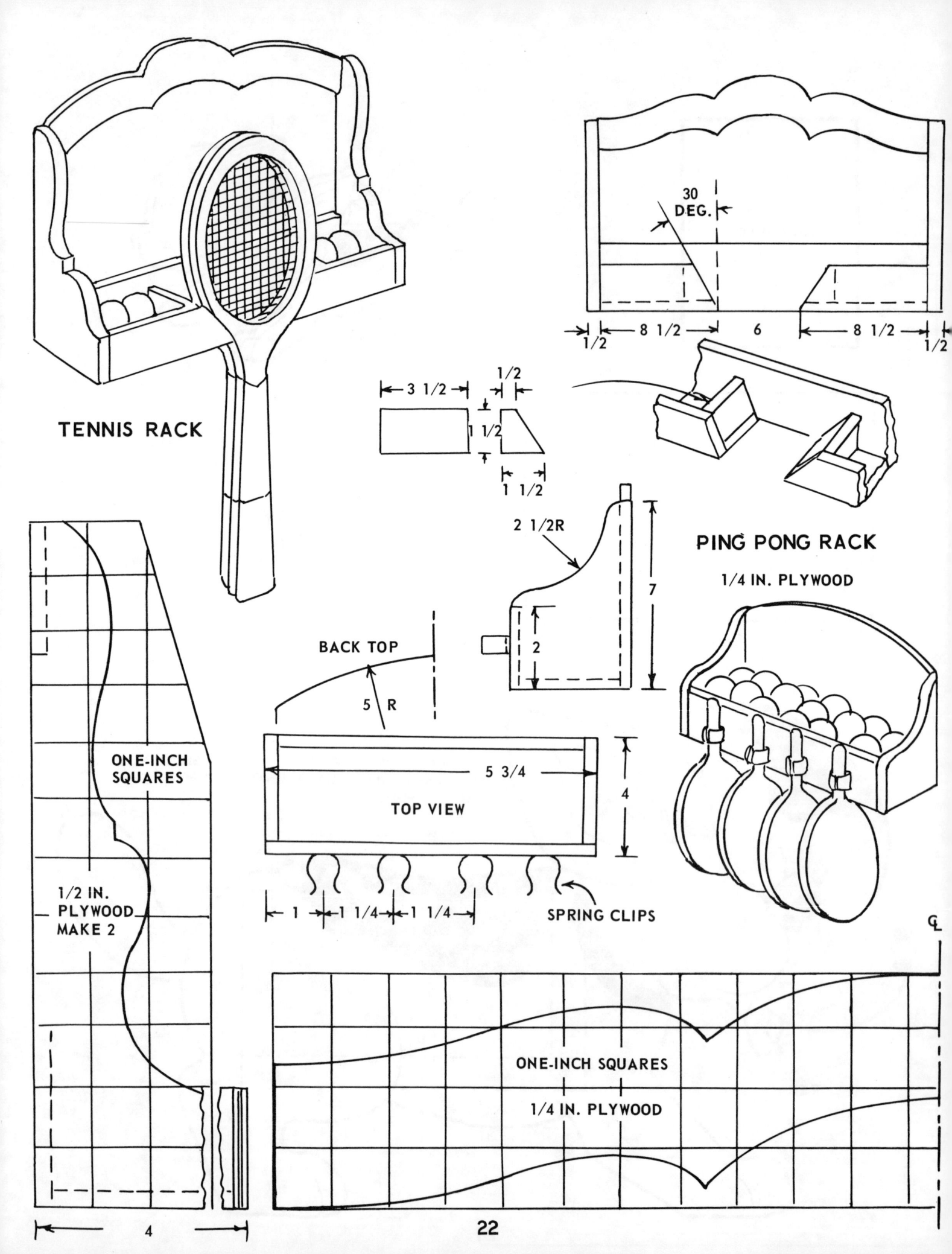

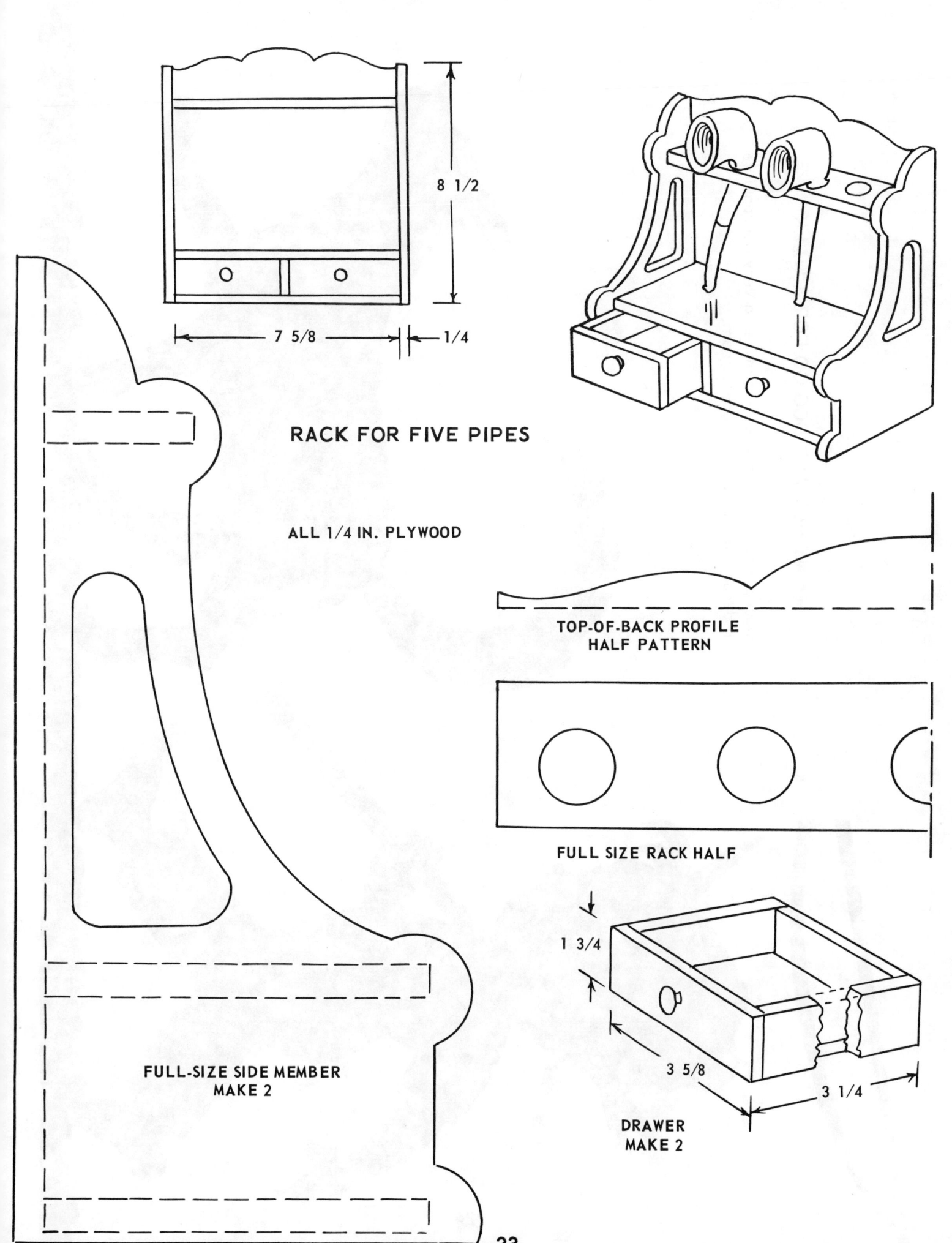

SONNY BOY AND DOG GO FOR A WALK

A plaque made from this pattern makes a very appropriate wall decoration for a small boy's room.

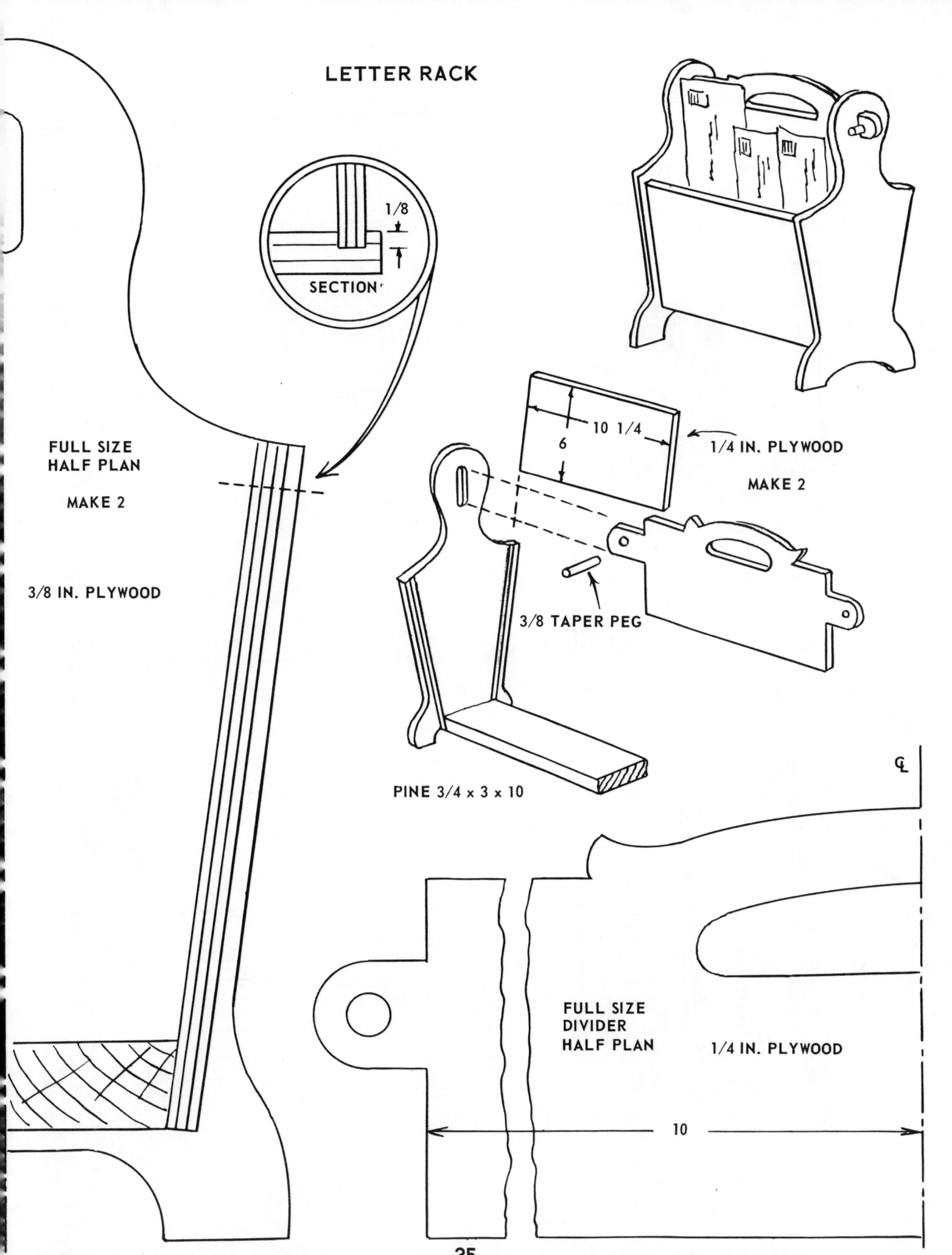

DETAIL SHOWING JOINT ASSEMBLY – THIS IS USED ON ALL SHADOW BOX SHELVES

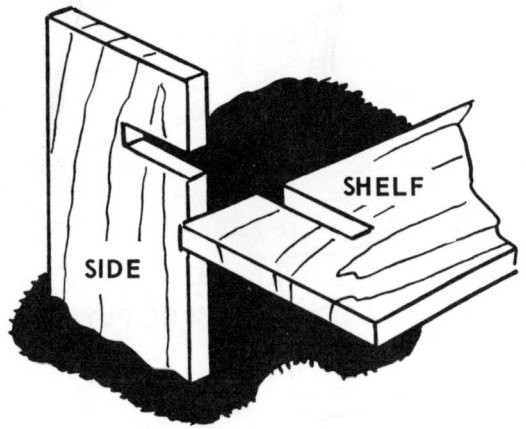

HALF-LAP JOINT

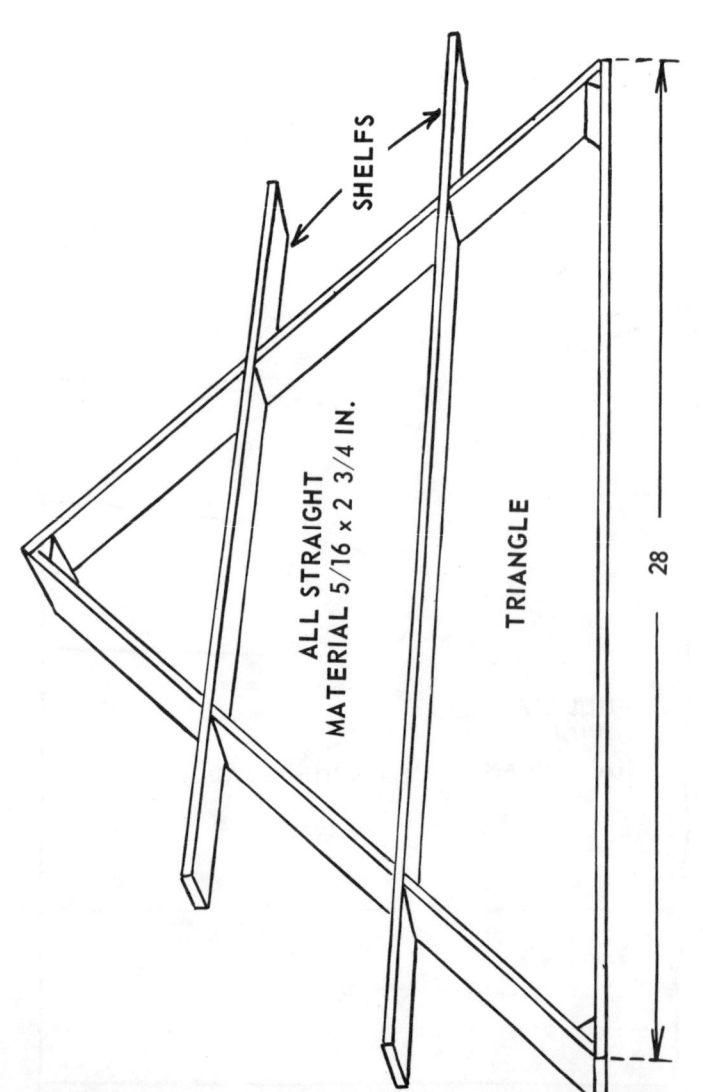

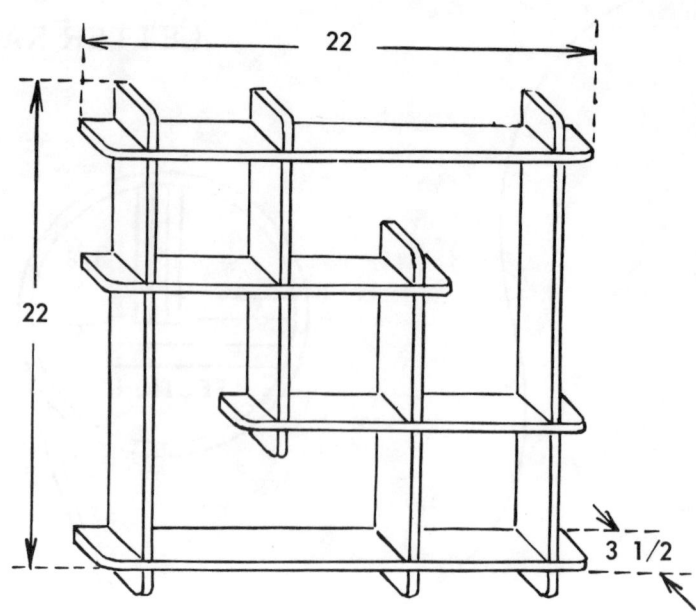

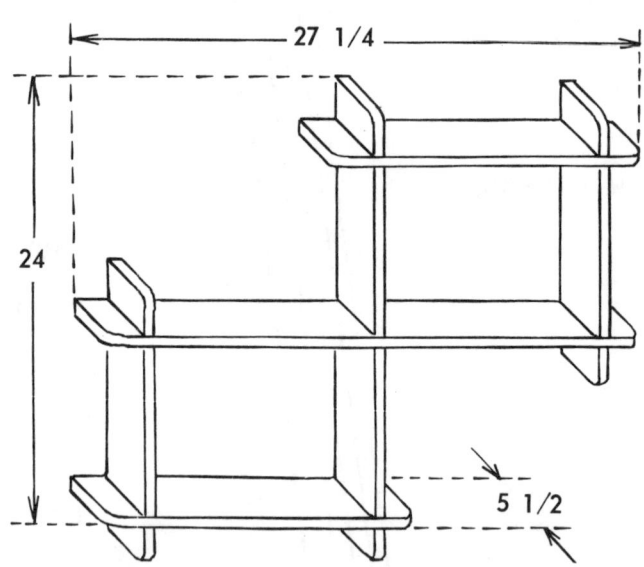

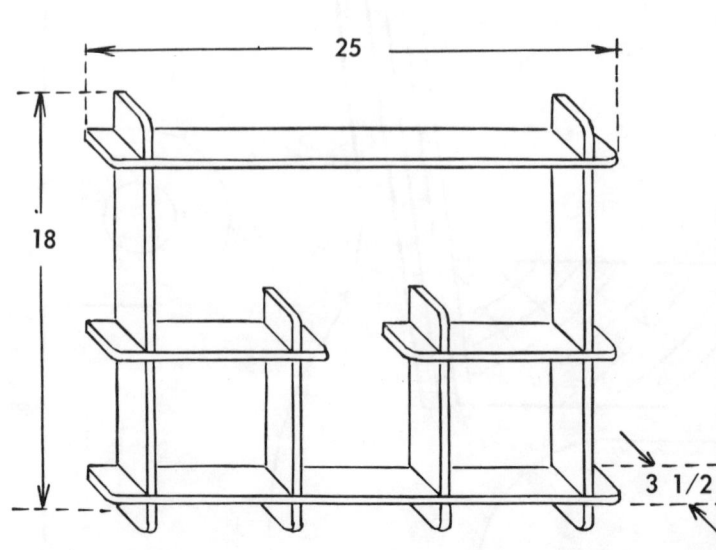

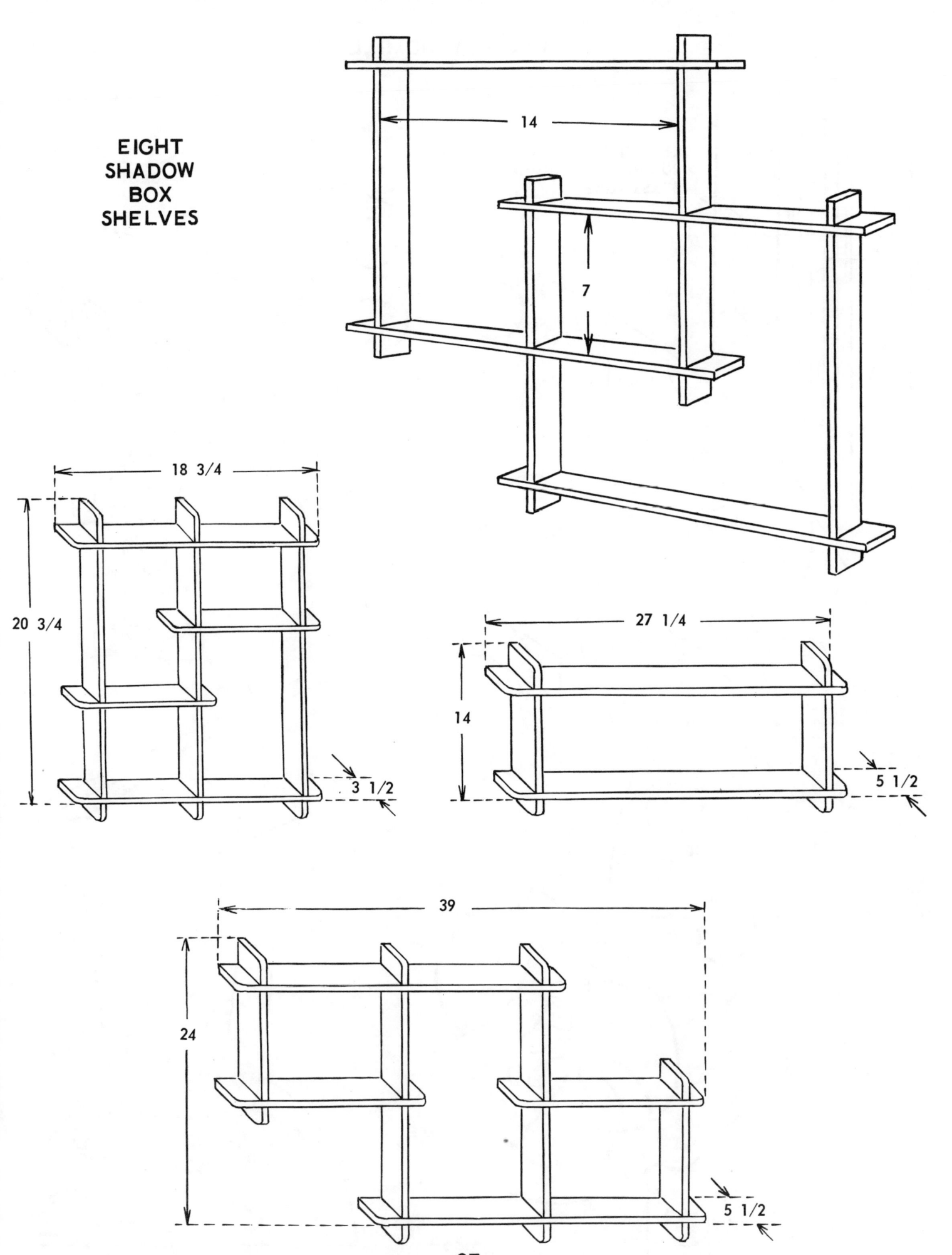

CLOWN WINDMILL

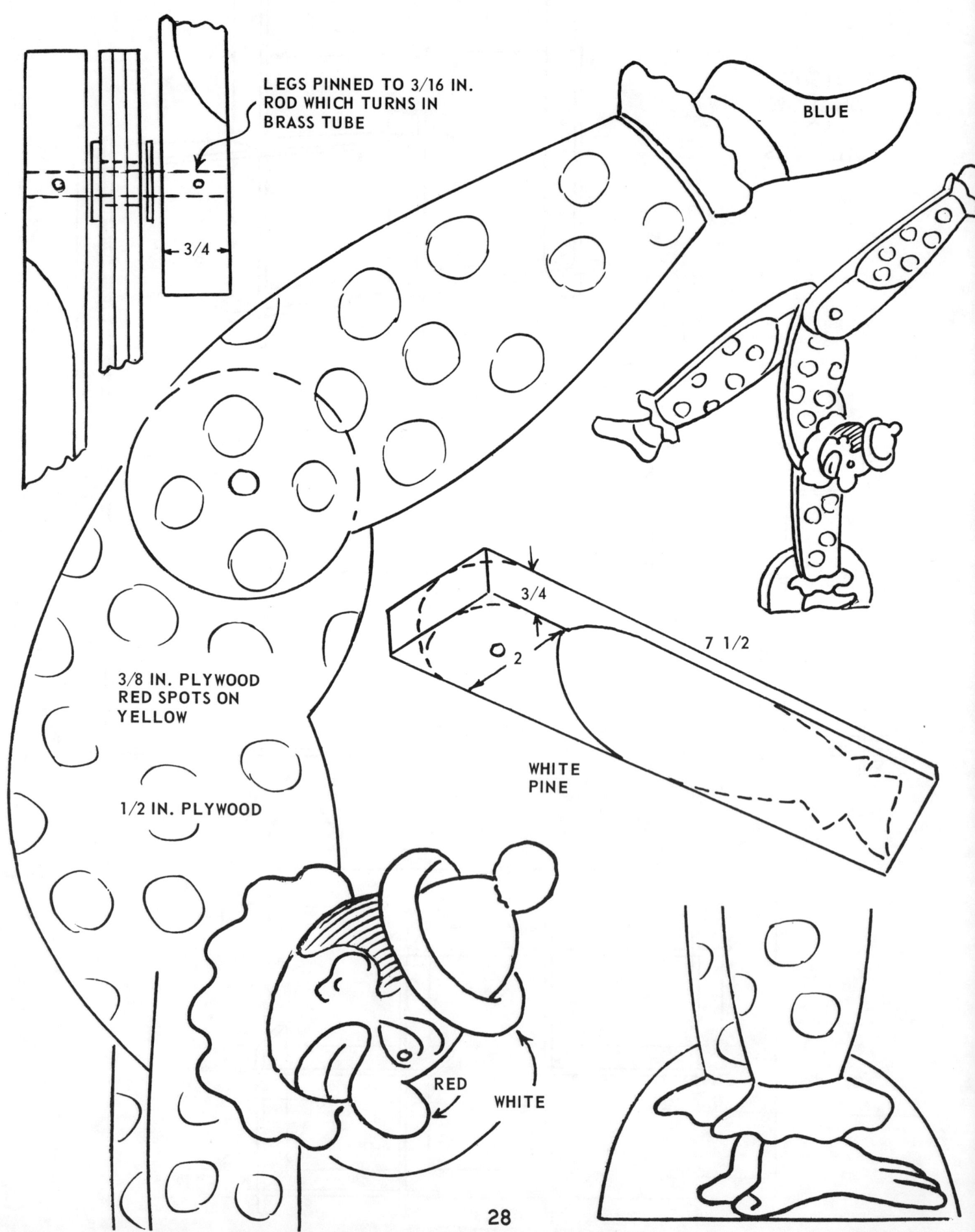

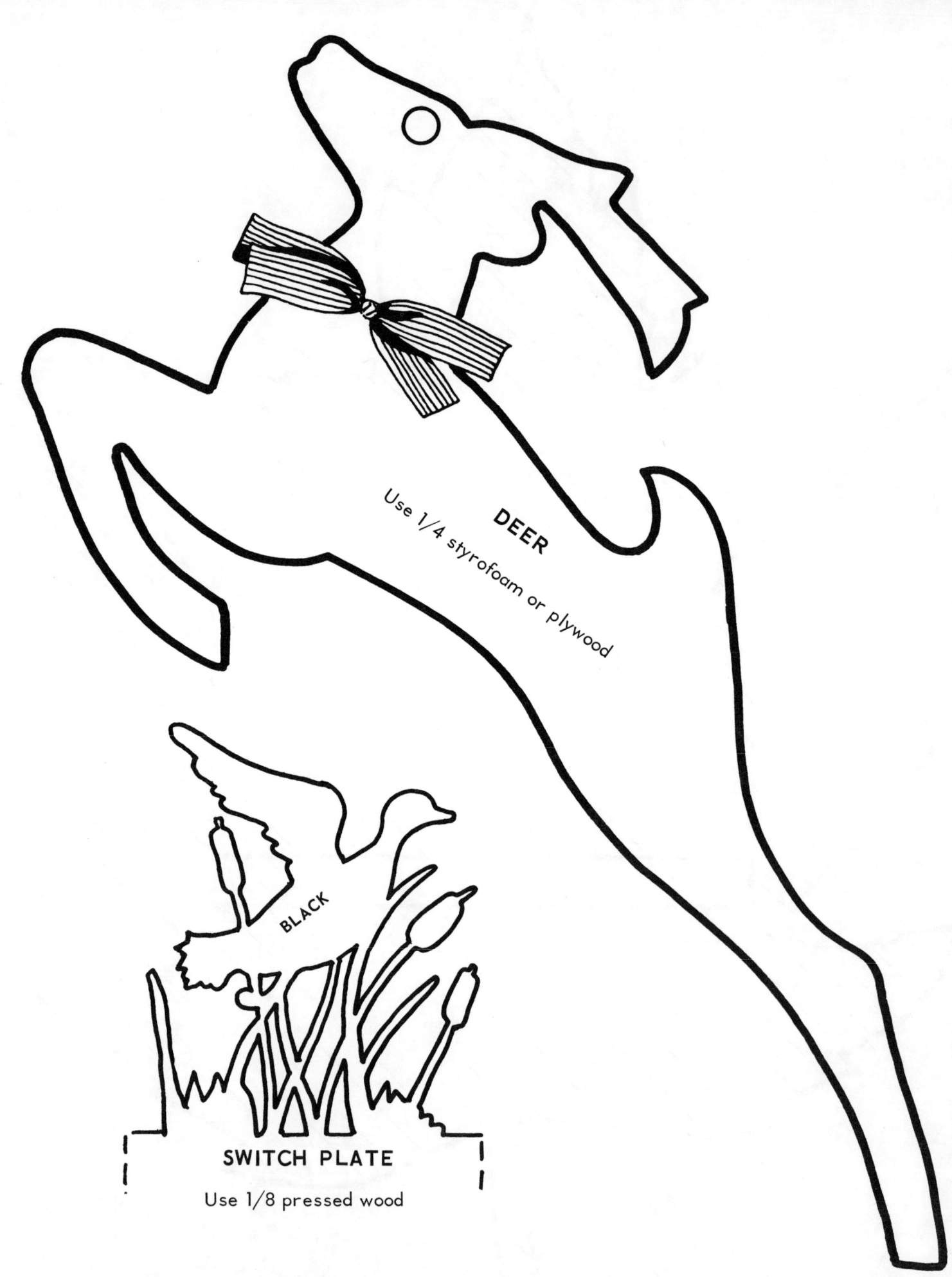

ABCDEFGHIJ
KLMN OPQR
STUVWXYZ

Distinctive alphabet letters you can use to personalize costumes and make initial pins. See page 54 for information on attaching pin backs.

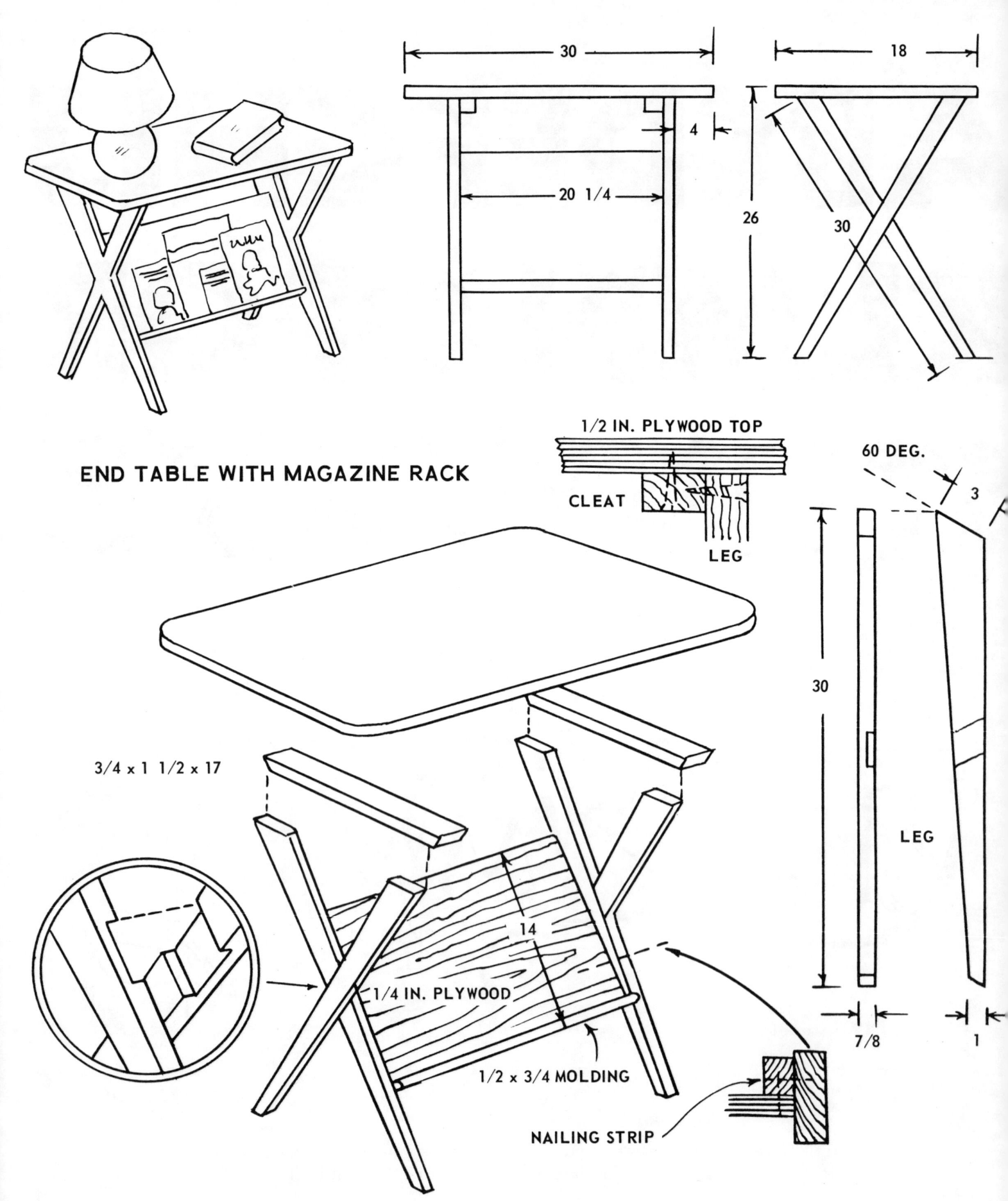

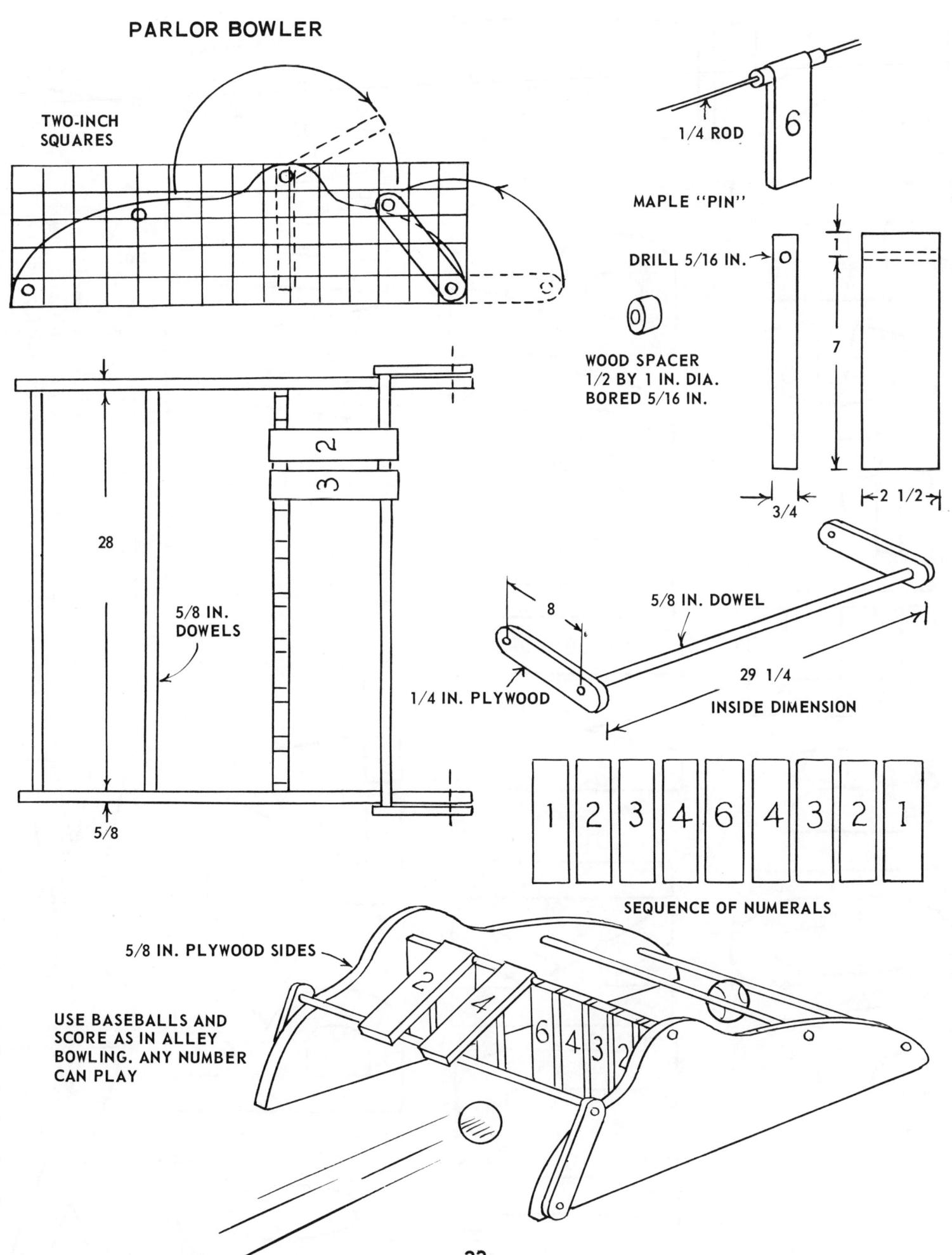

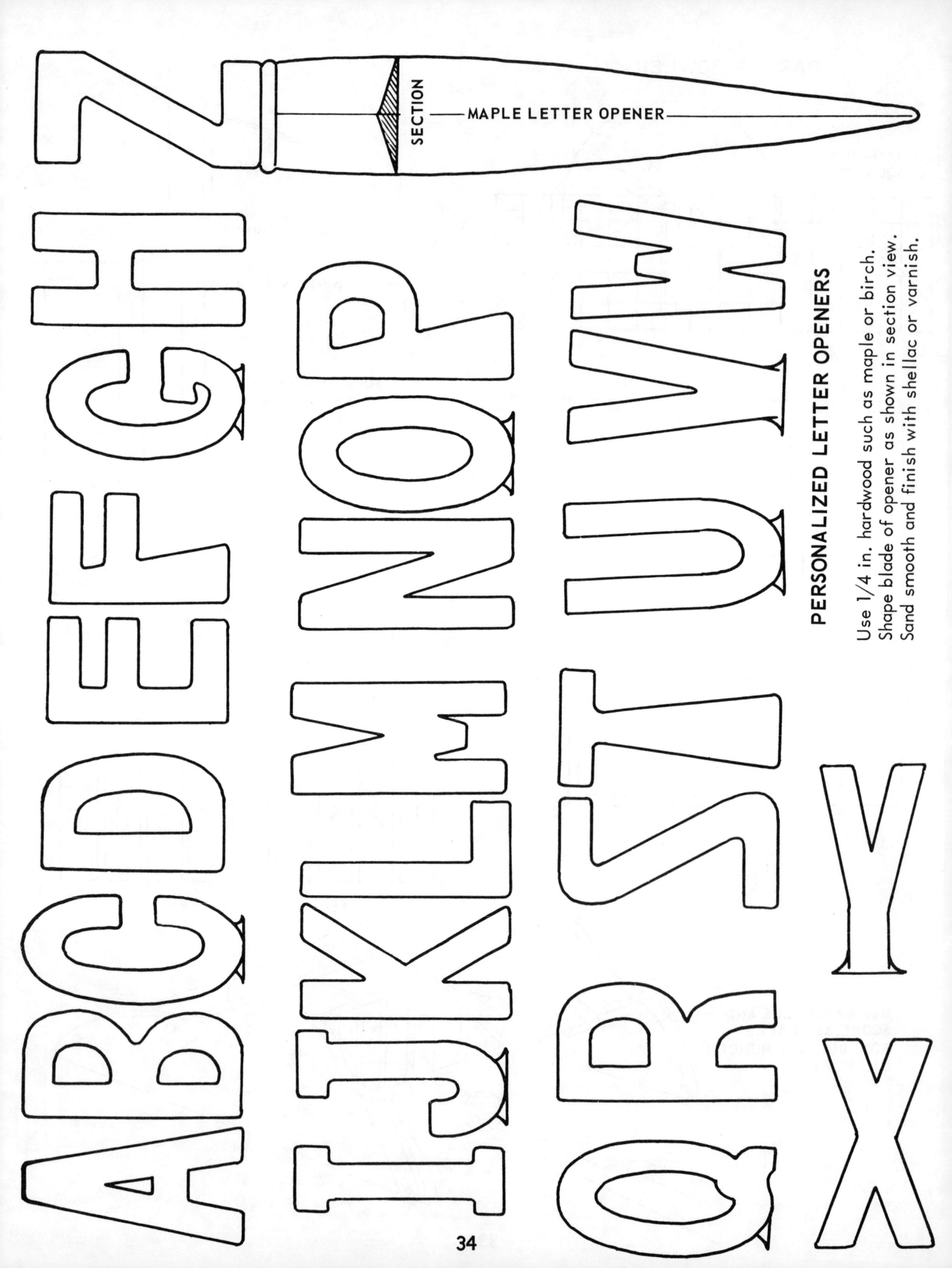

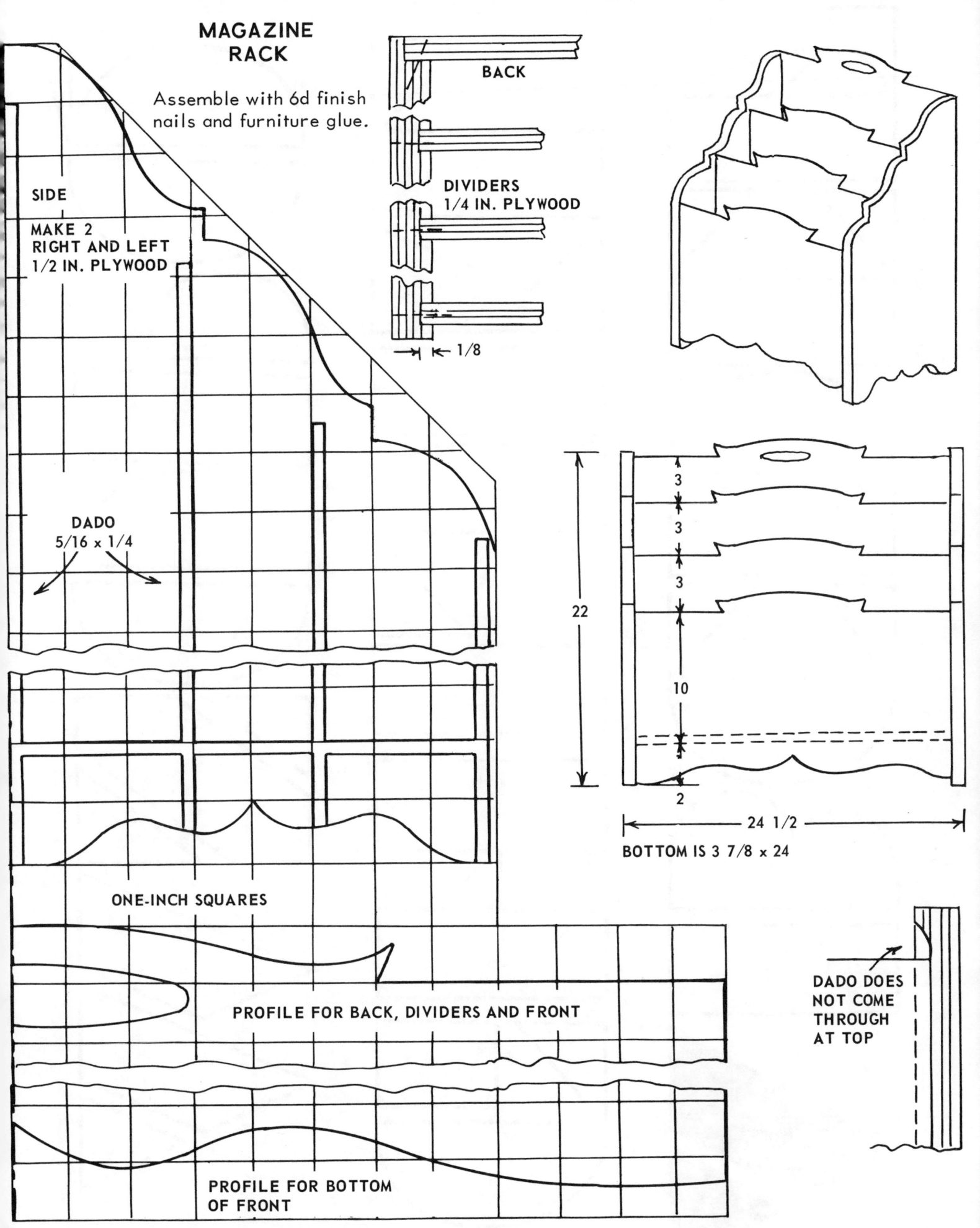

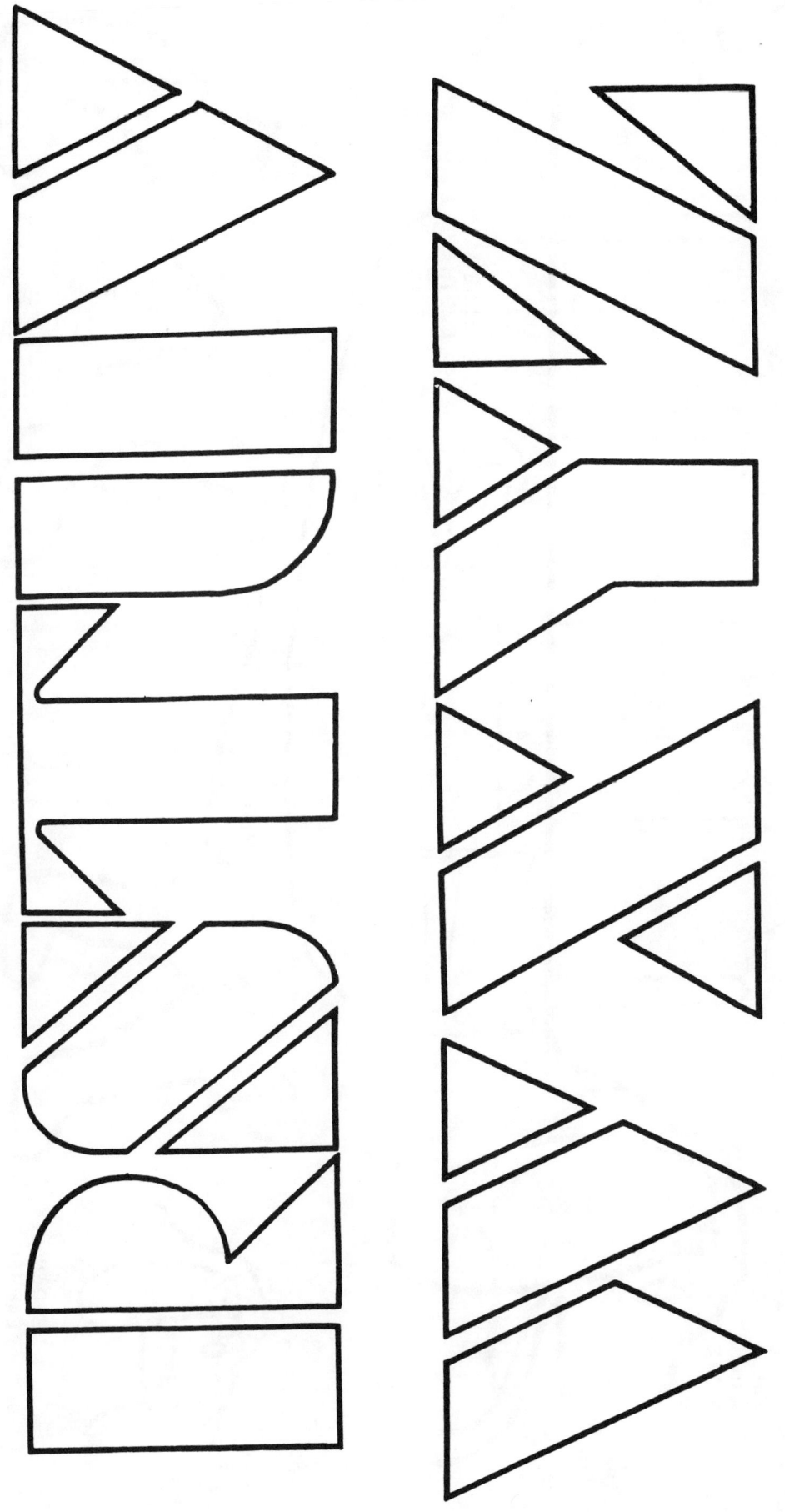

MODERN ALPHABET

With these alphabet letters you can personalize craft projects, make store and desk name signs, letter show cards...do many other lettering jobs.

SEWING GADGET

Here is a cute project you can make in a short time. 3/4 in. plywood is suggested. Be sure to put a peg on the tail to take a thimble. A base 3/4 in. stock, 4 in. wide and 10 in. long is needed.

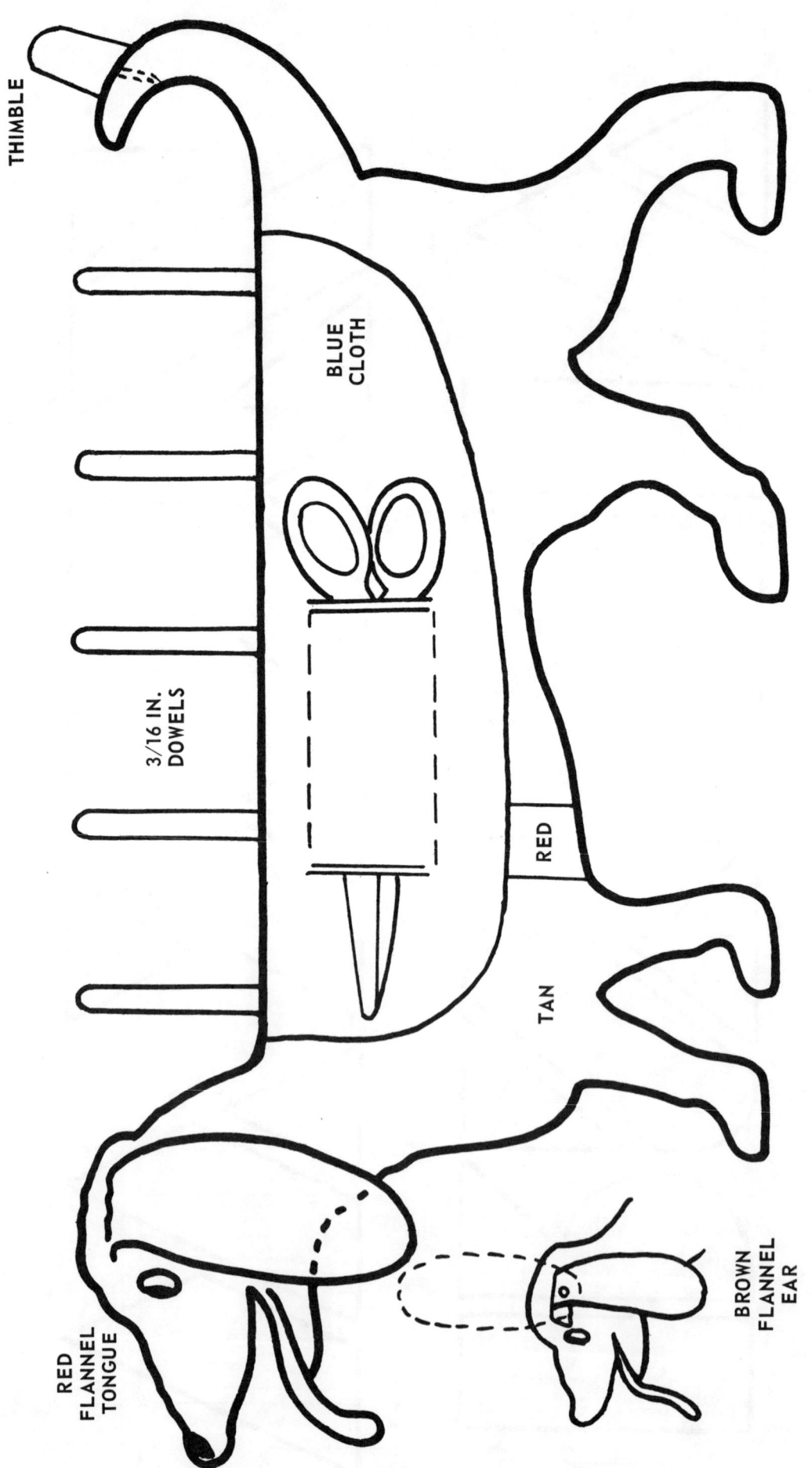

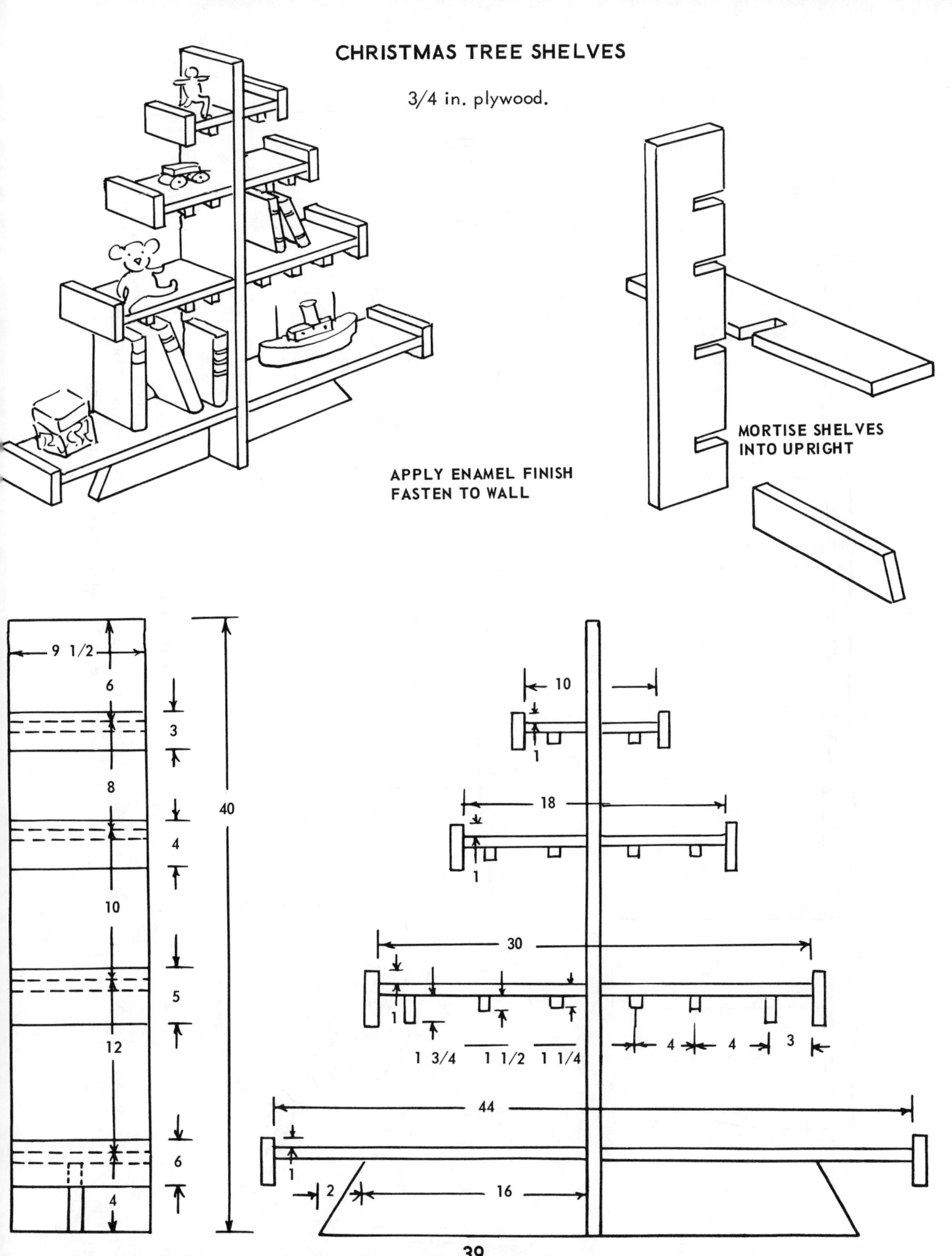

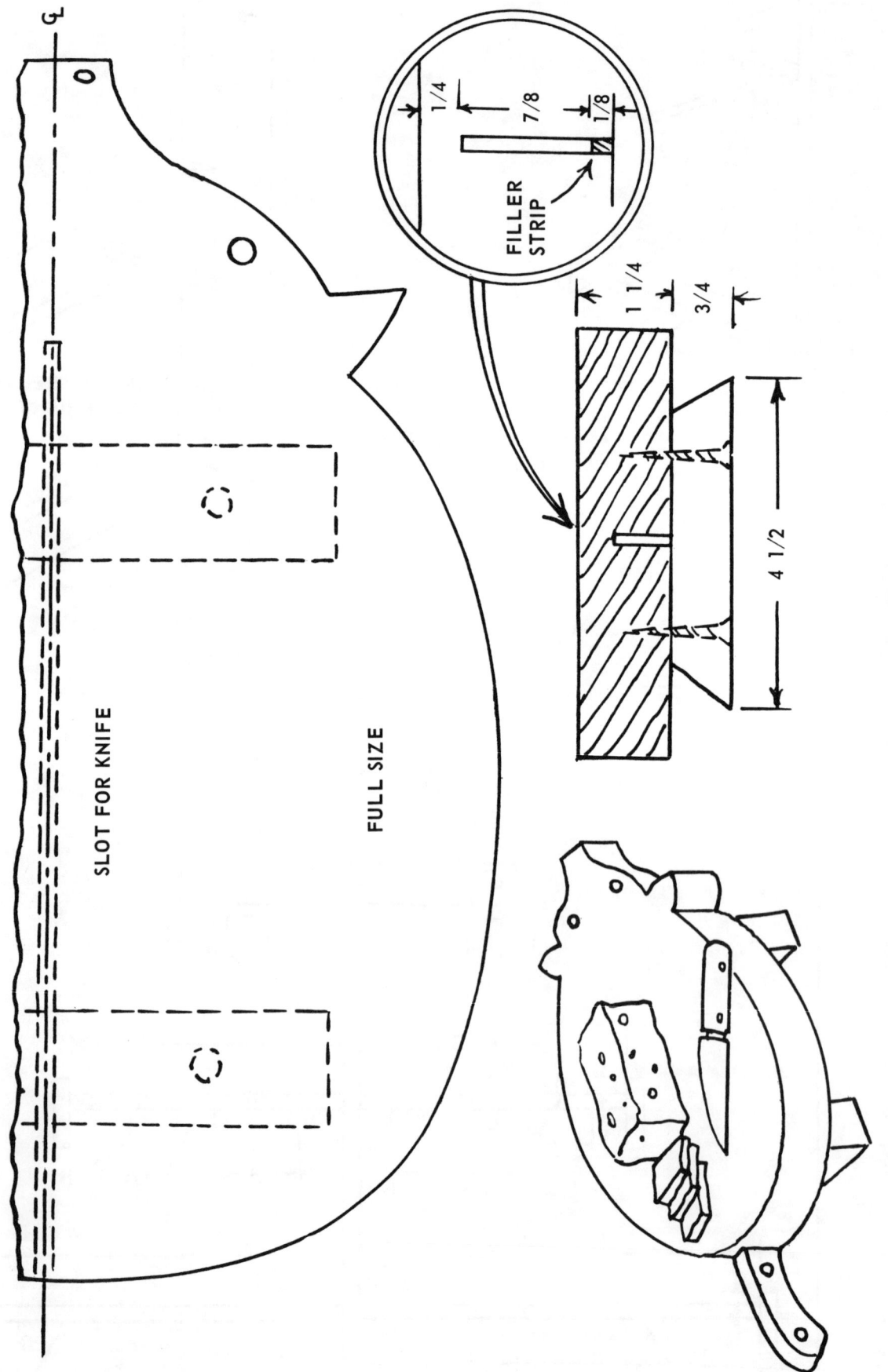

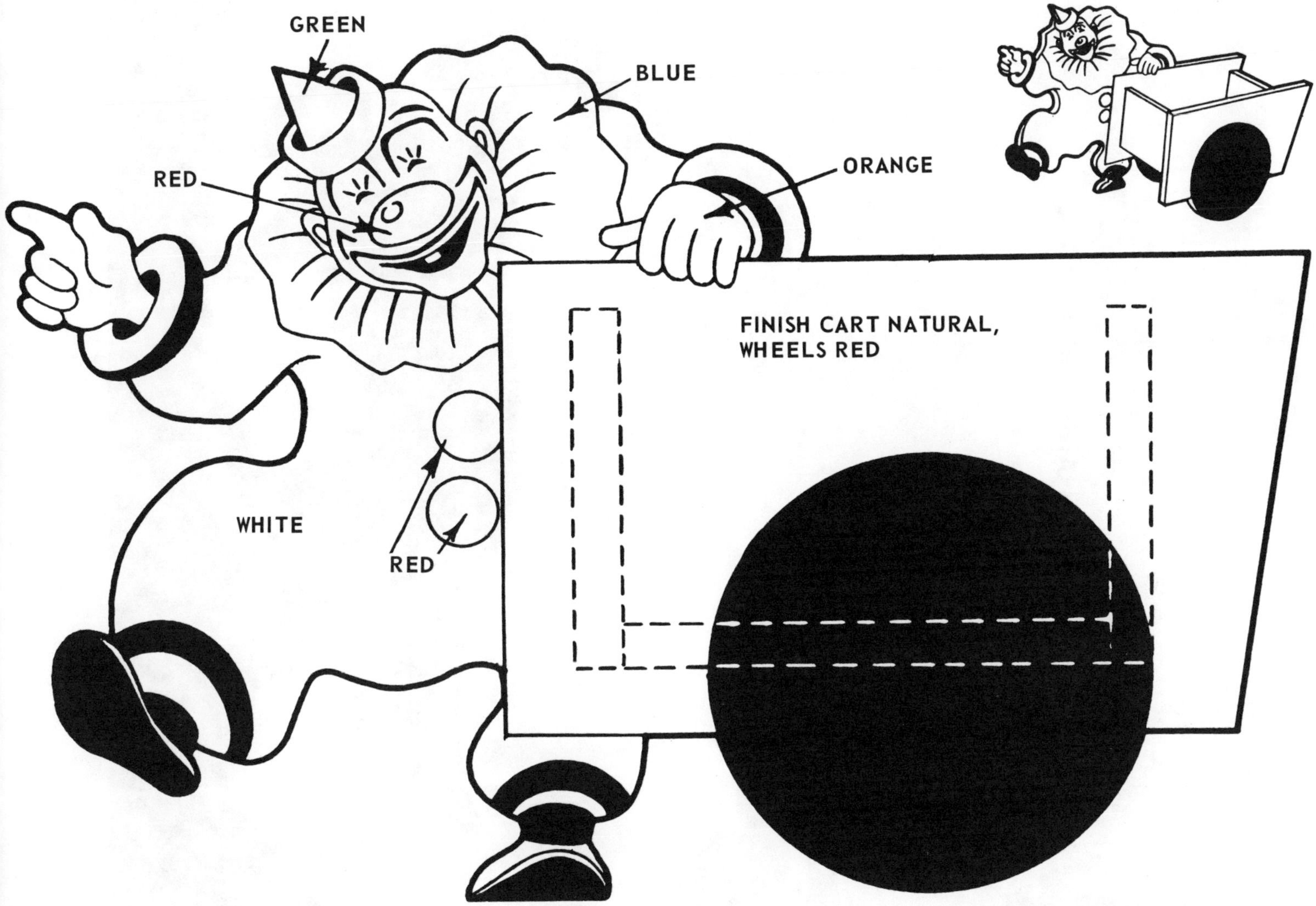

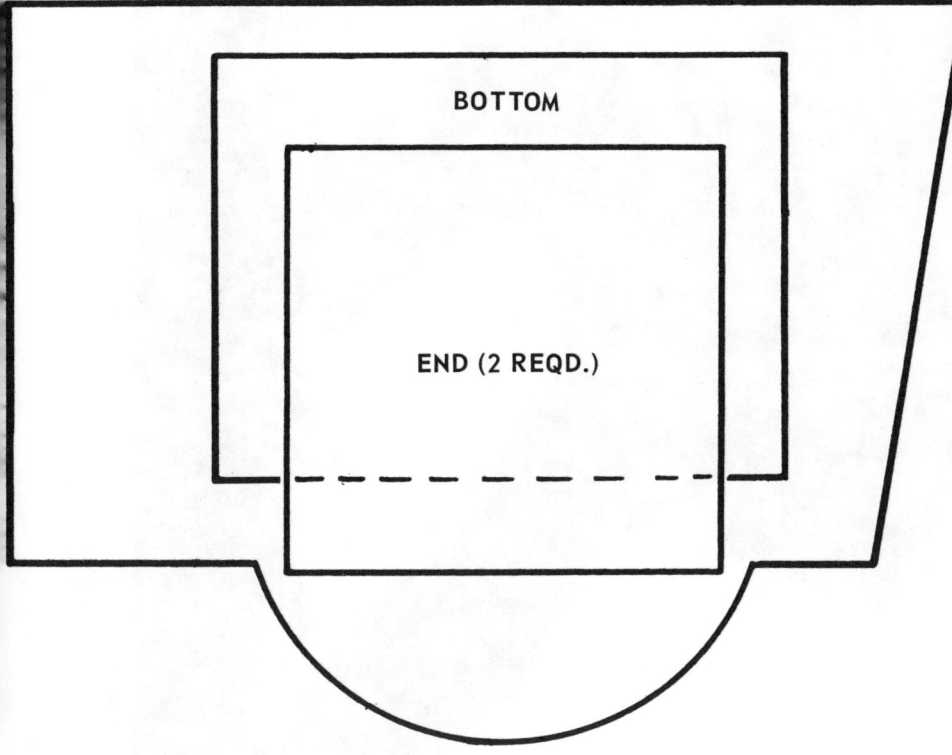

COLORFUL CLOWN PLANTER BOX

Material suggested, 3/8 in. solid stock for bottom and ends; 1/4 in. plywood for other pieces. Fit pieces accurately, assemble with 1 1/4 in. wire brads and waterproof glue. Coat with spar varnish, paint on design, give inside of box two more coats of spar varnish. When watering plants try to keep from getting water on edges and outside of flower box.

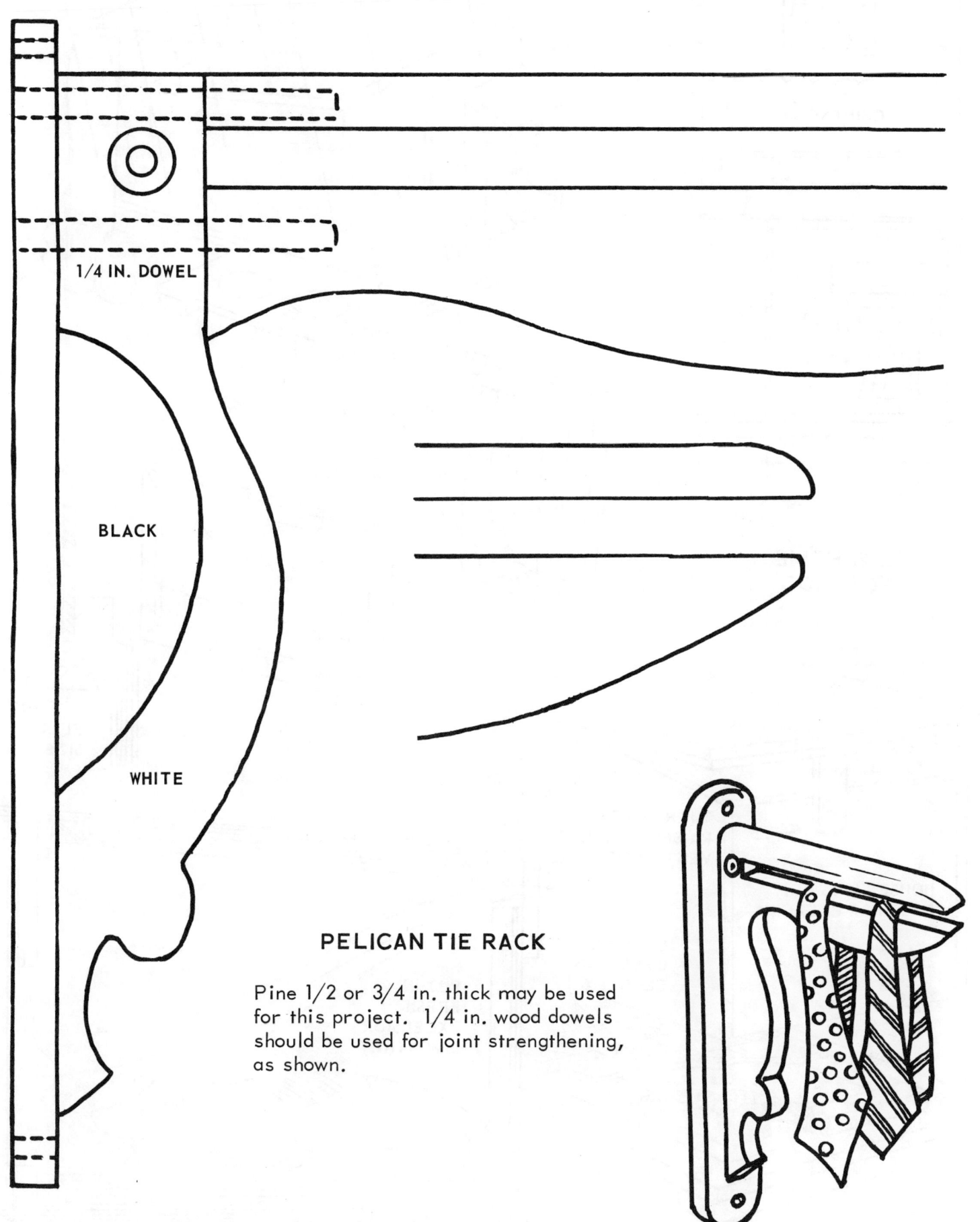

PELICAN TIE RACK

Pine 1/2 or 3/4 in. thick may be used for this project. 1/4 in. wood dowels should be used for joint strengthening, as shown.

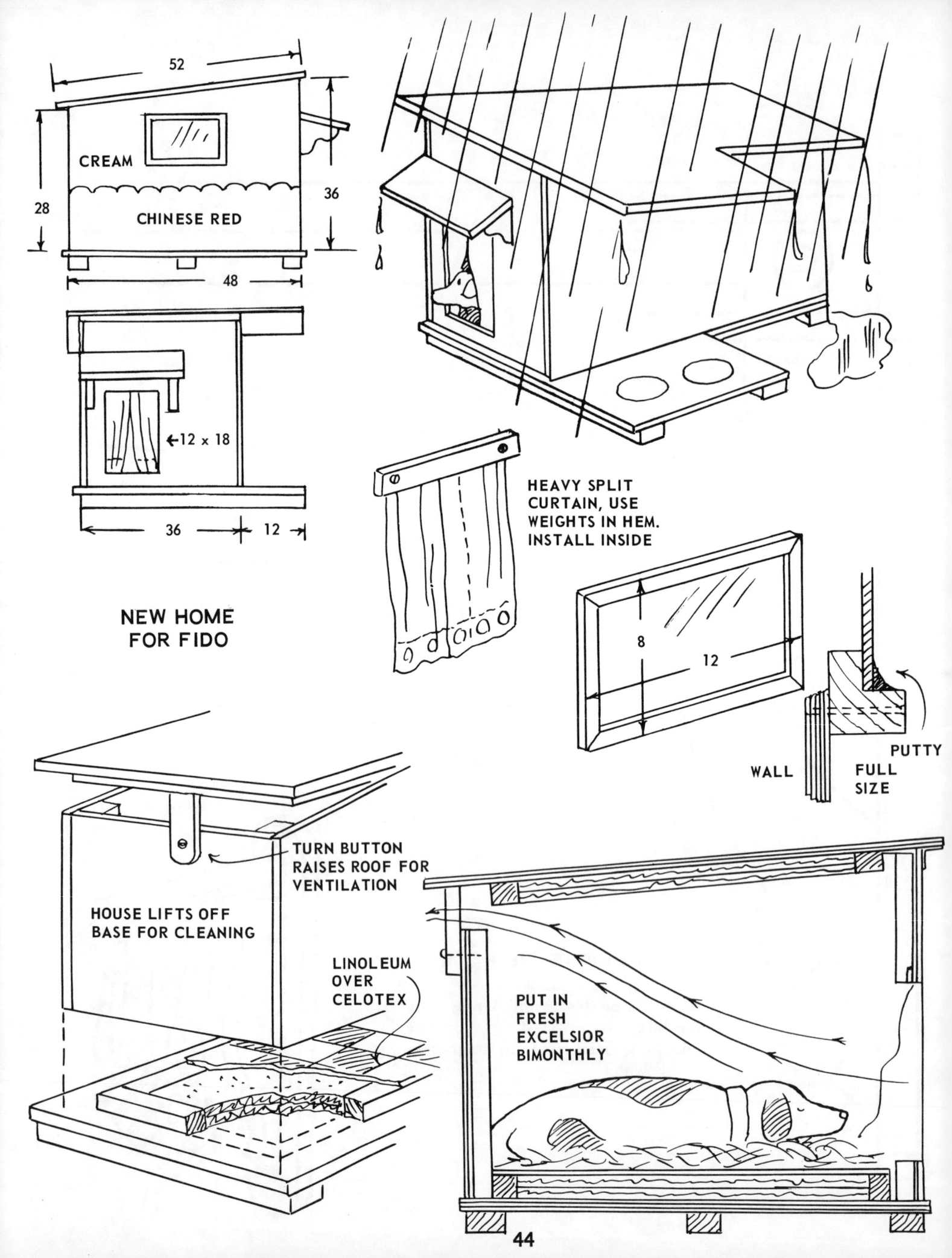

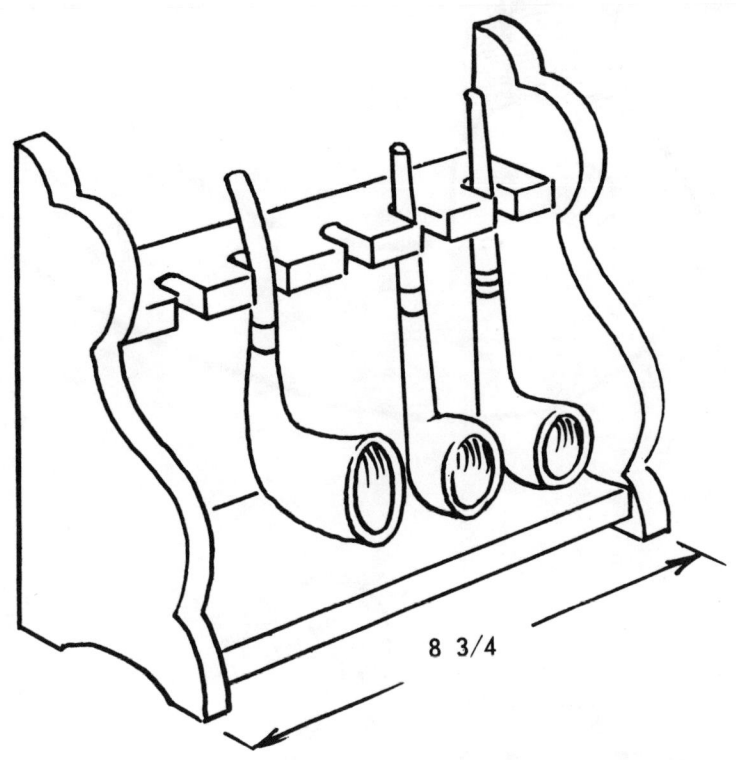

PIPE RACK

Solid stock, mahogany or walnut, is suggested for this project. Assemble with 1 in. wire brads and glue.

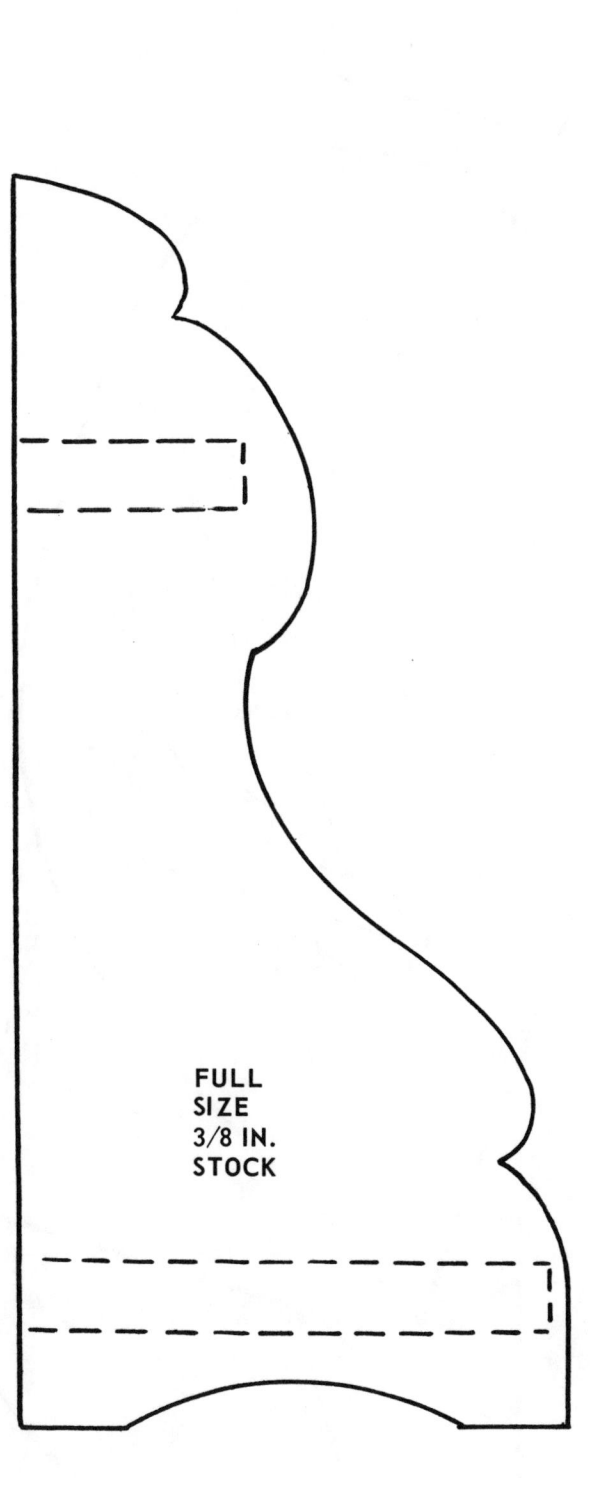

FULL SIZE
3/8 IN. STOCK

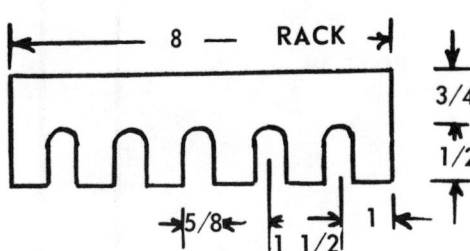

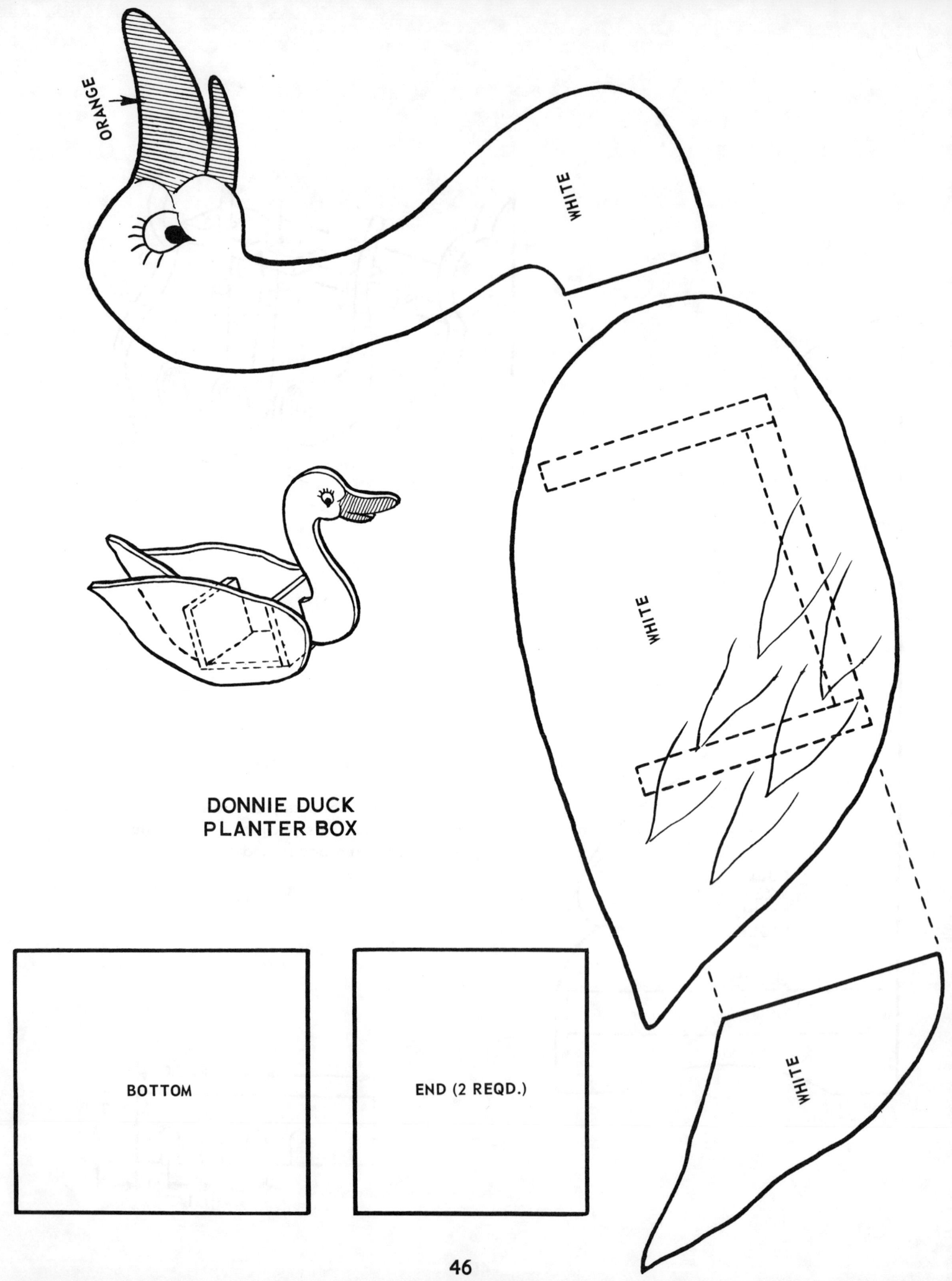

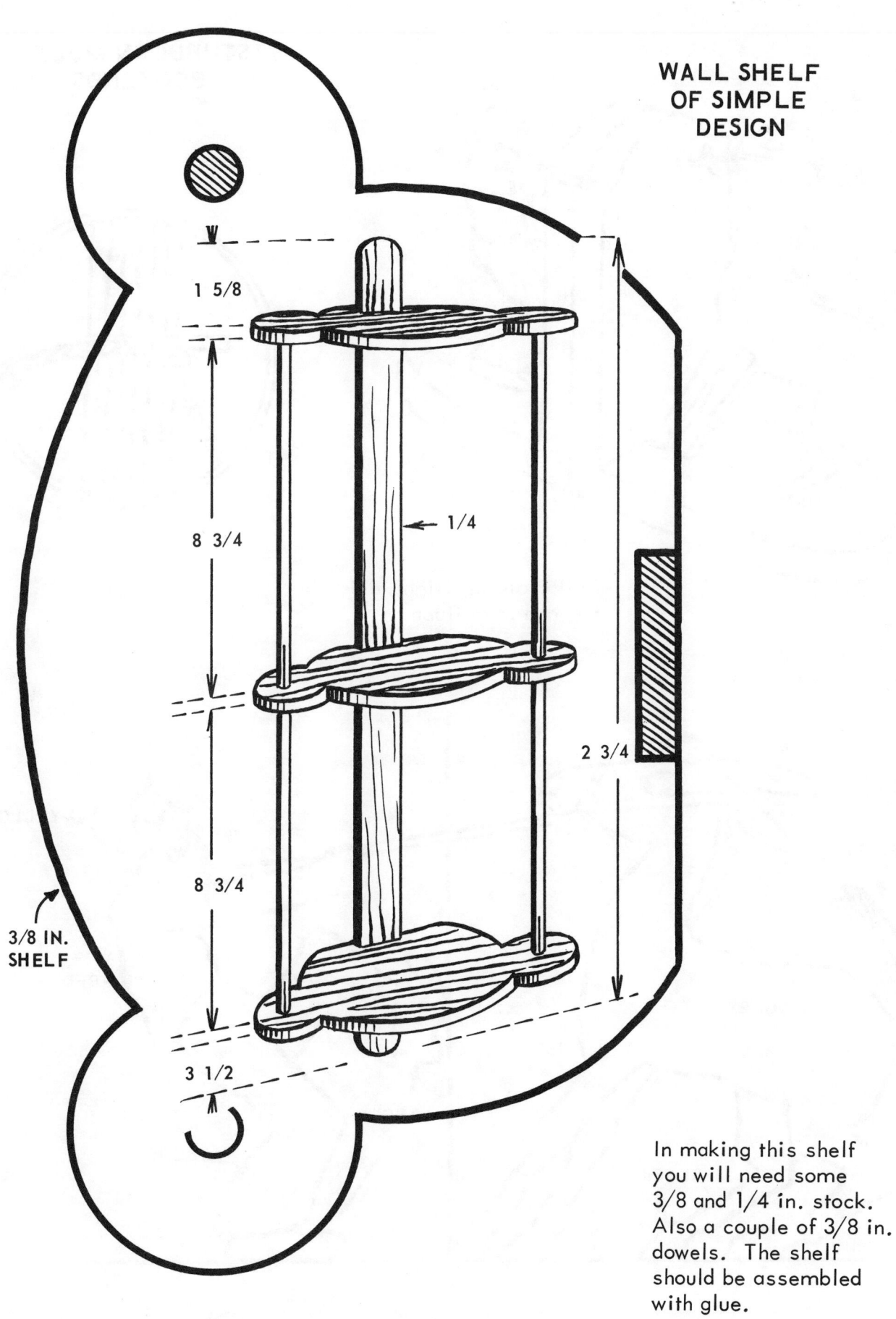

WALL SHELF OF SIMPLE DESIGN

In making this shelf you will need some 3/8 and 1/4 in. stock. Also a couple of 3/8 in. dowels. The shelf should be assembled with glue.

STUBBORN MULE BOOKENDS

Pull chalk line tight, drive in peg and trim flush

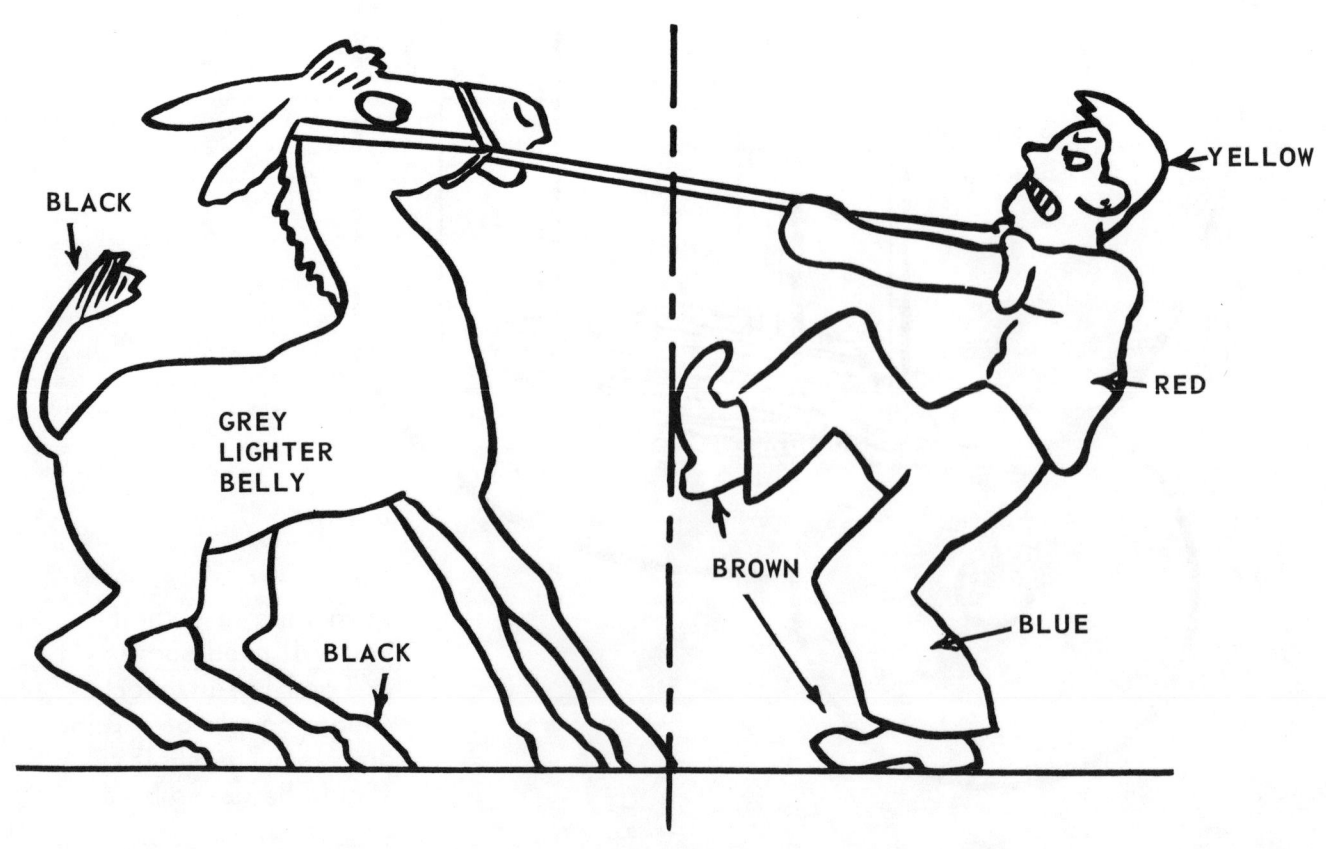

48

ABCDEFGHIJK
LMNOPQRSTUVW
XYZ

abcdefghijklm
nopqrstuvwxyz

NAME PINS MAKE PERSONALIZED GIFTS THAT ARE SURE TO BE APPRECIATED

Material suggested: 1/4 in. plywood or solid stock. Bar at top of name may be omitted if plywood is used. See page 54 for information on attaching pin backs.

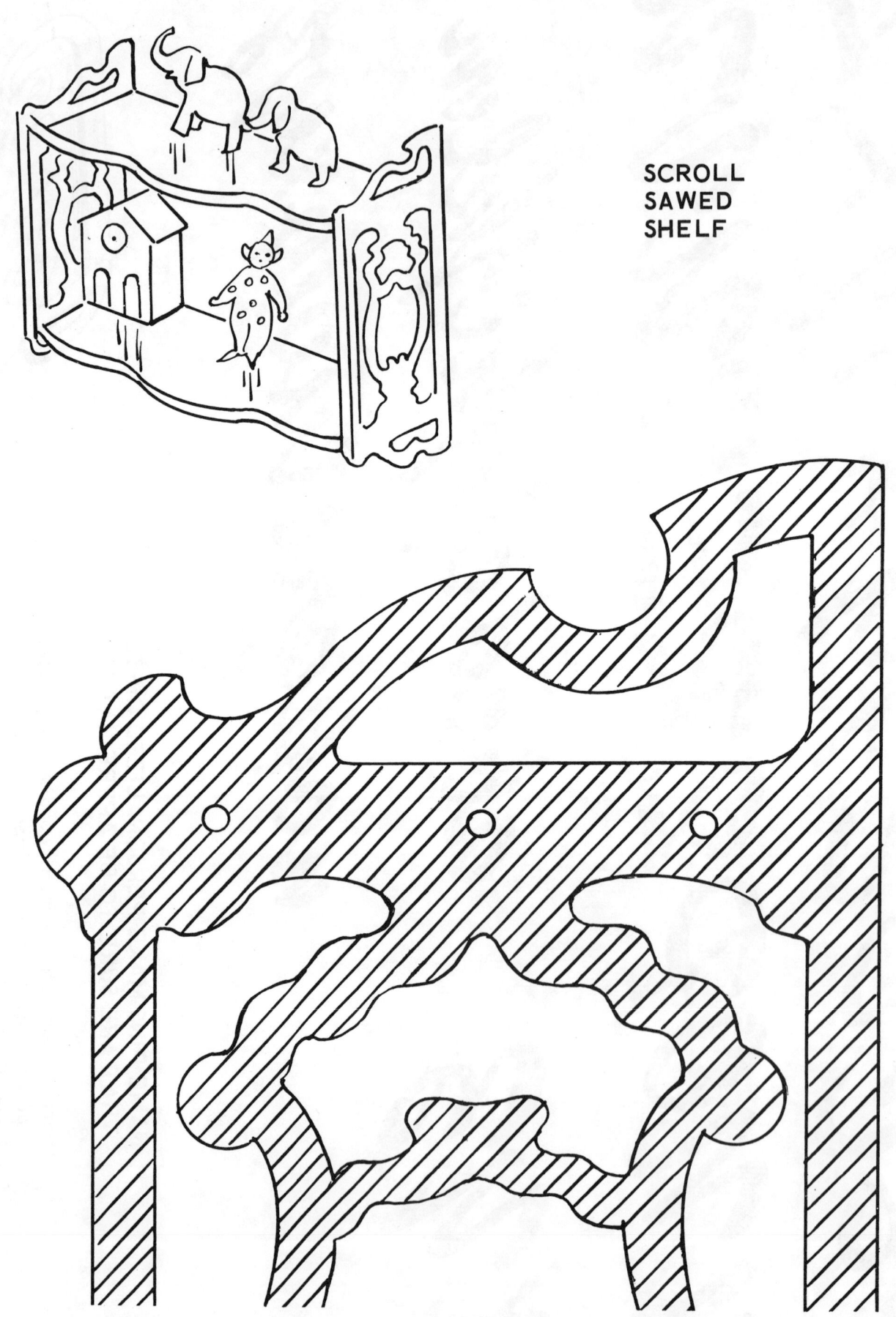

SCROLL SAWED SHELF

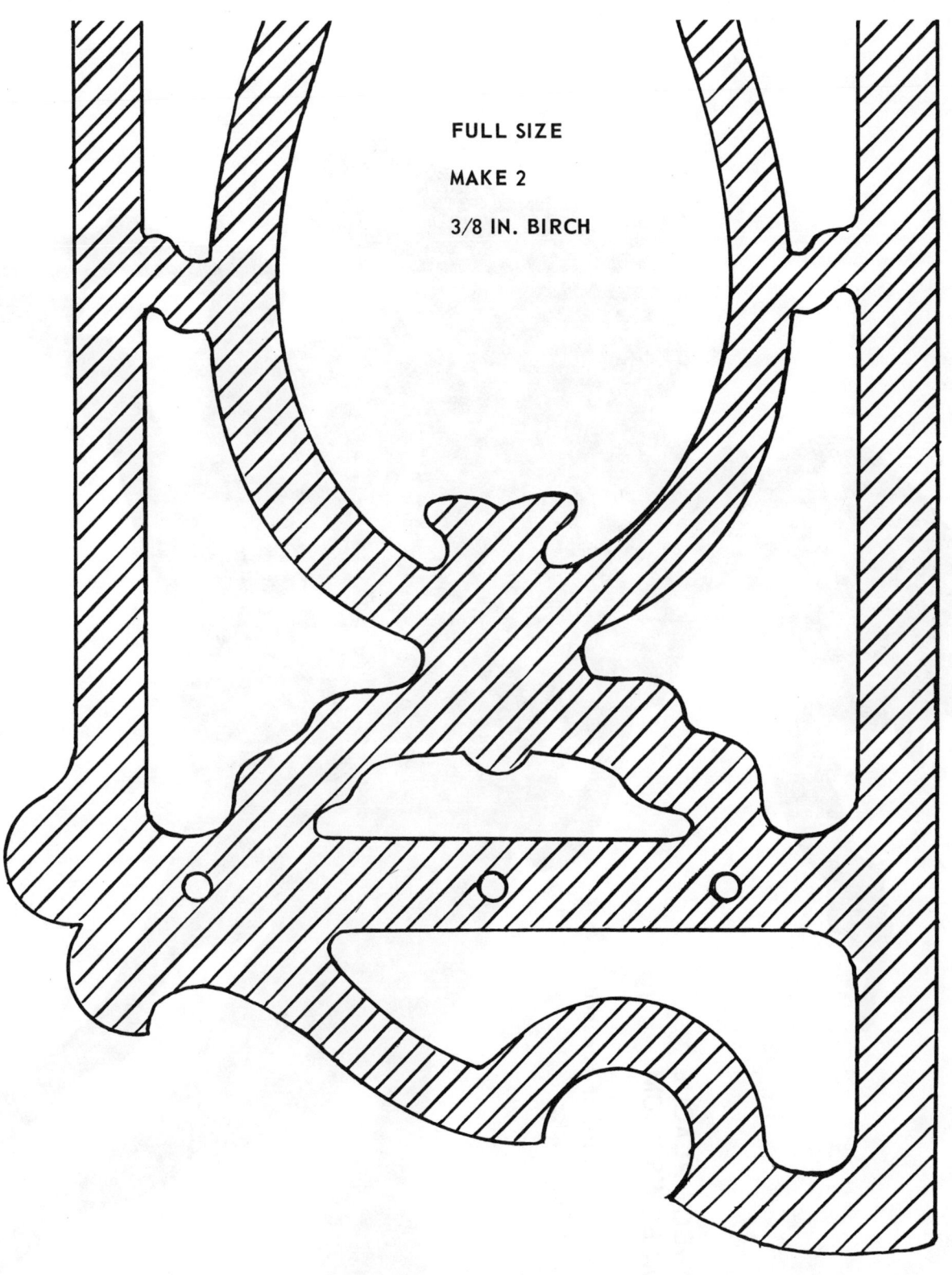

FULL SIZE

MAKE 2

3/8 IN. BIRCH

In making this shelf you can be sure both sides are identical if you cut both at the same time. Two pieces of wood may be held together temporarily by using small wire brads. Suggested shelf size 3/8 x 5 1/2 x 22.

COWBOY PLAQUE FOR BOY'S ROOM

1/4 or 1/2 in. plywood or pressed wood. Paint flat black.

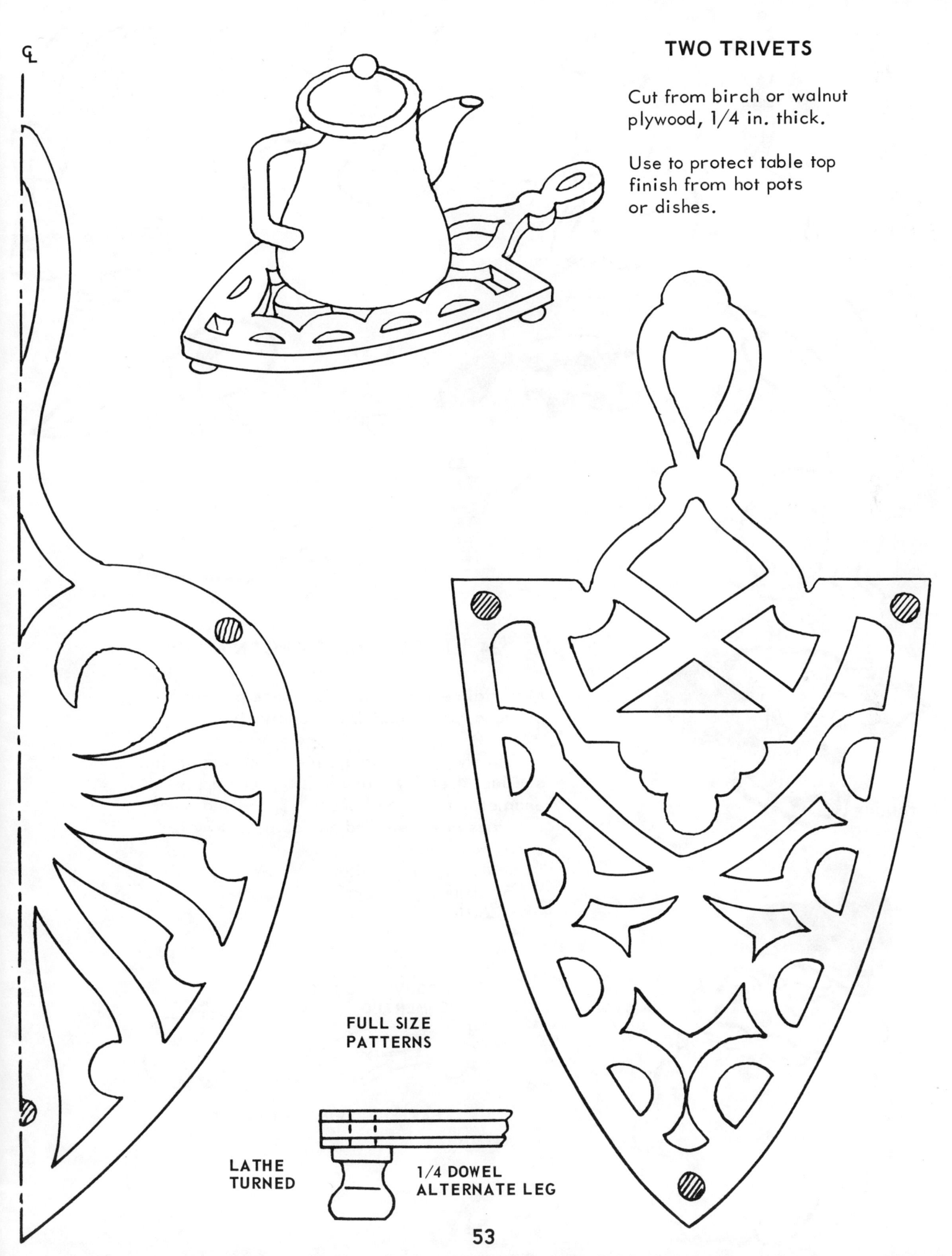

TWO TRIVETS

Cut from birch or walnut plywood, 1/4 in. thick.

Use to protect table top finish from hot pots or dishes.

FULL SIZE PATTERNS

LATHE TURNED

1/4 DOWEL ALTERNATE LEG

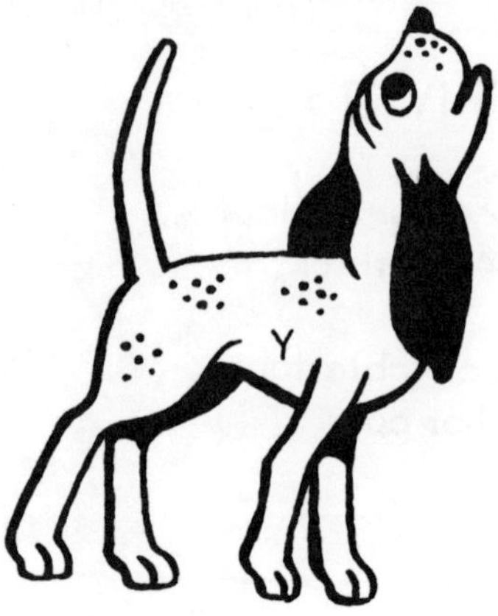
Y

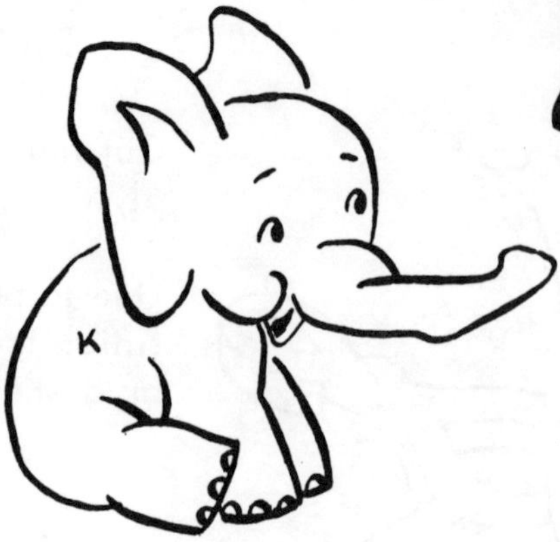
K

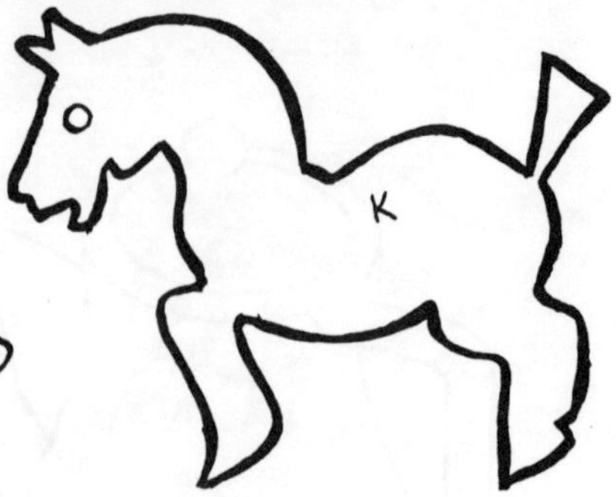
K

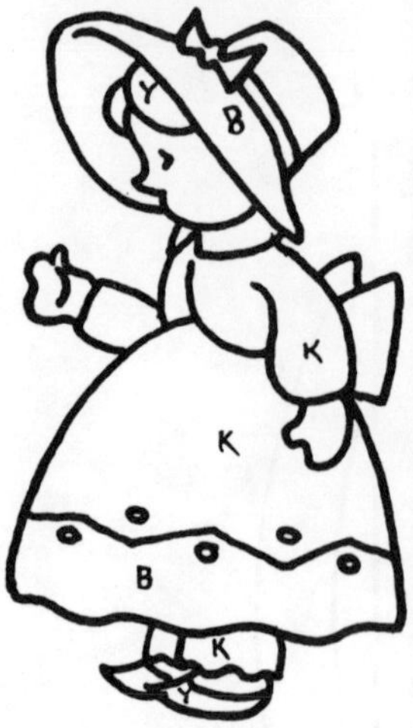
Y
B
K
K
B
K
Y

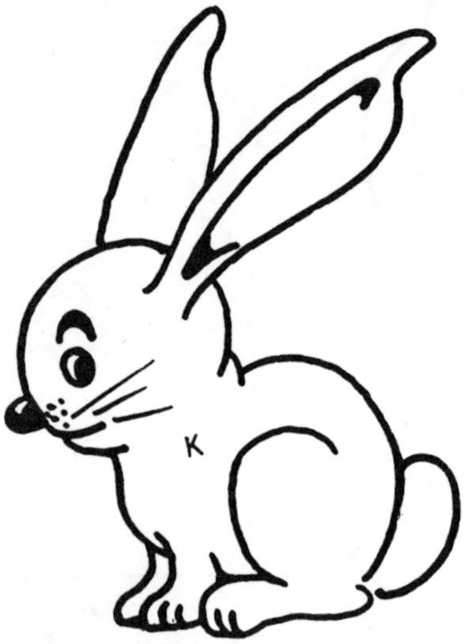
K

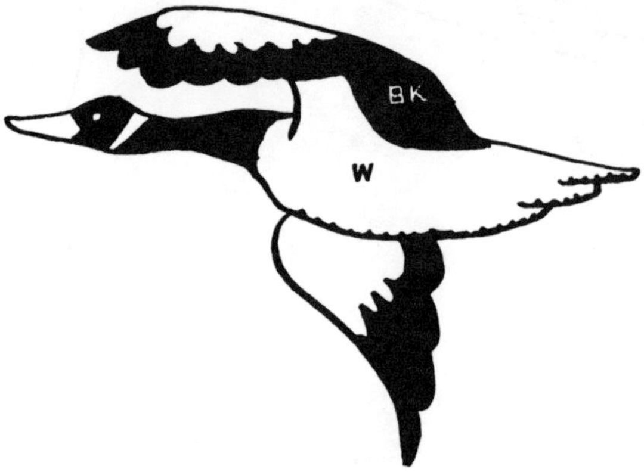
BK
W

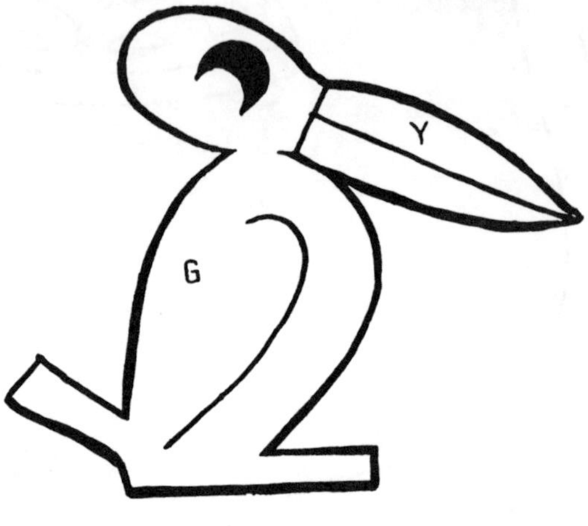
Y
G

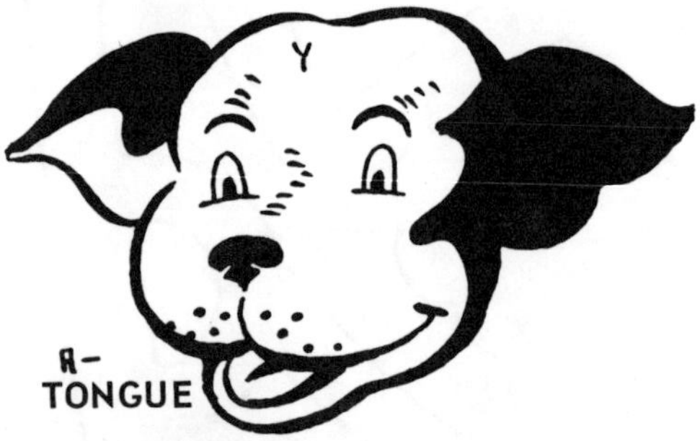
Y
R-
TONGUE

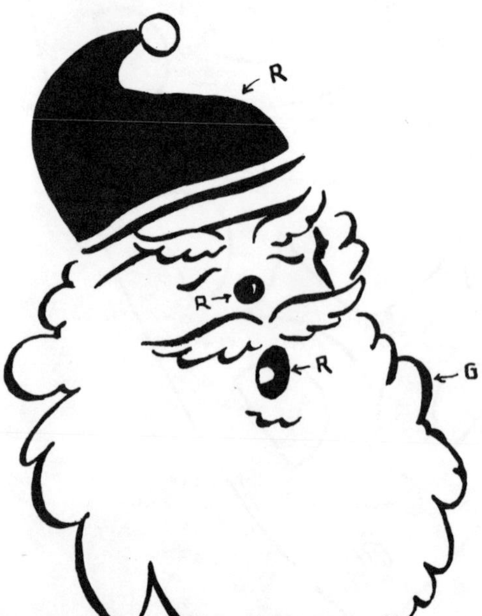
R
R
R
G

24 LAPEL PINS YOU CAN MAKE

Material recommended for these pins is 1/8 in. plywood, preferably birch or maple.

Saw to shape indicated, give wood coat of thin shellac. Let dry, sand lightly, then apply enamel, using small brush. Suggested color schemes are indicated on designs. Key to color schemes:

R - Red, Y - Yellow, W - White,
B - Blue, P - Purple, G - Green,
K - Pink

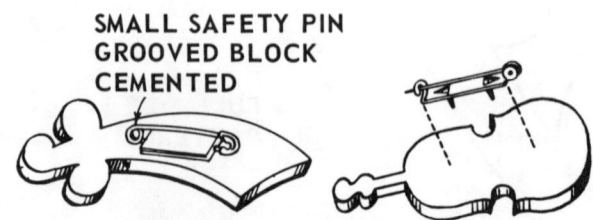

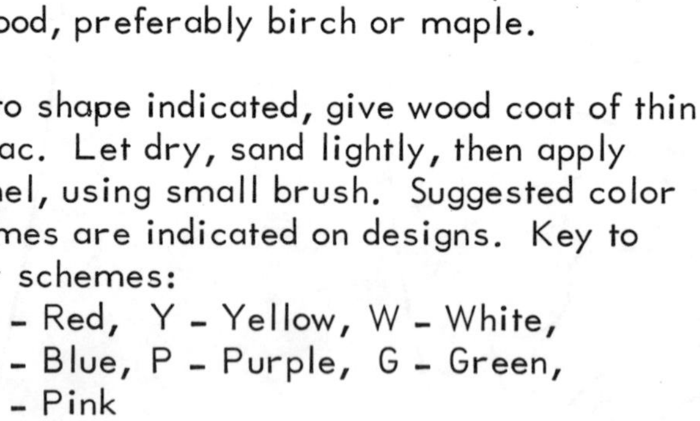
SMALL SAFETY PIN
GROOVED BLOCK
CEMENTED

FASTENING PINS ONTO WOOD

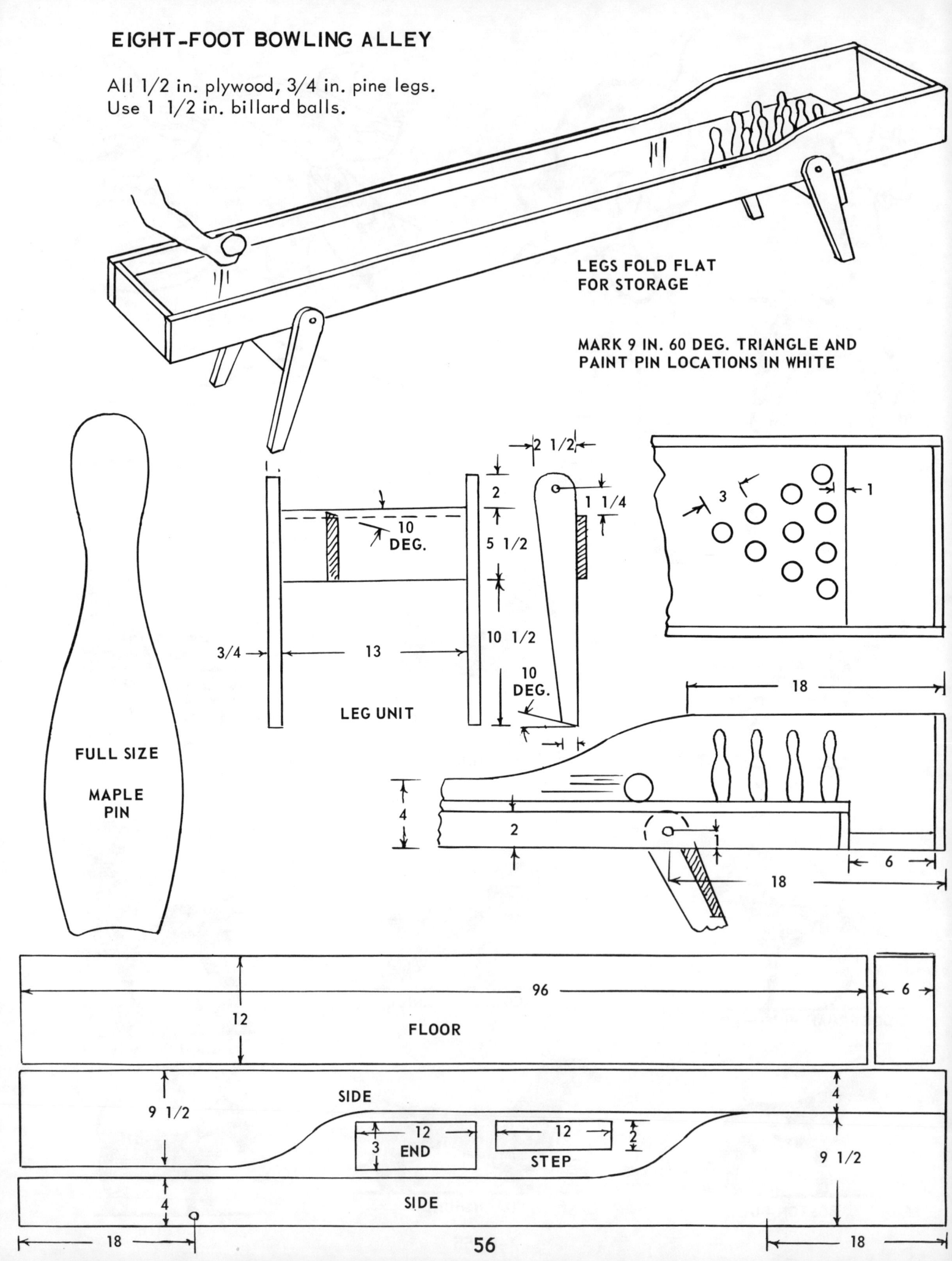

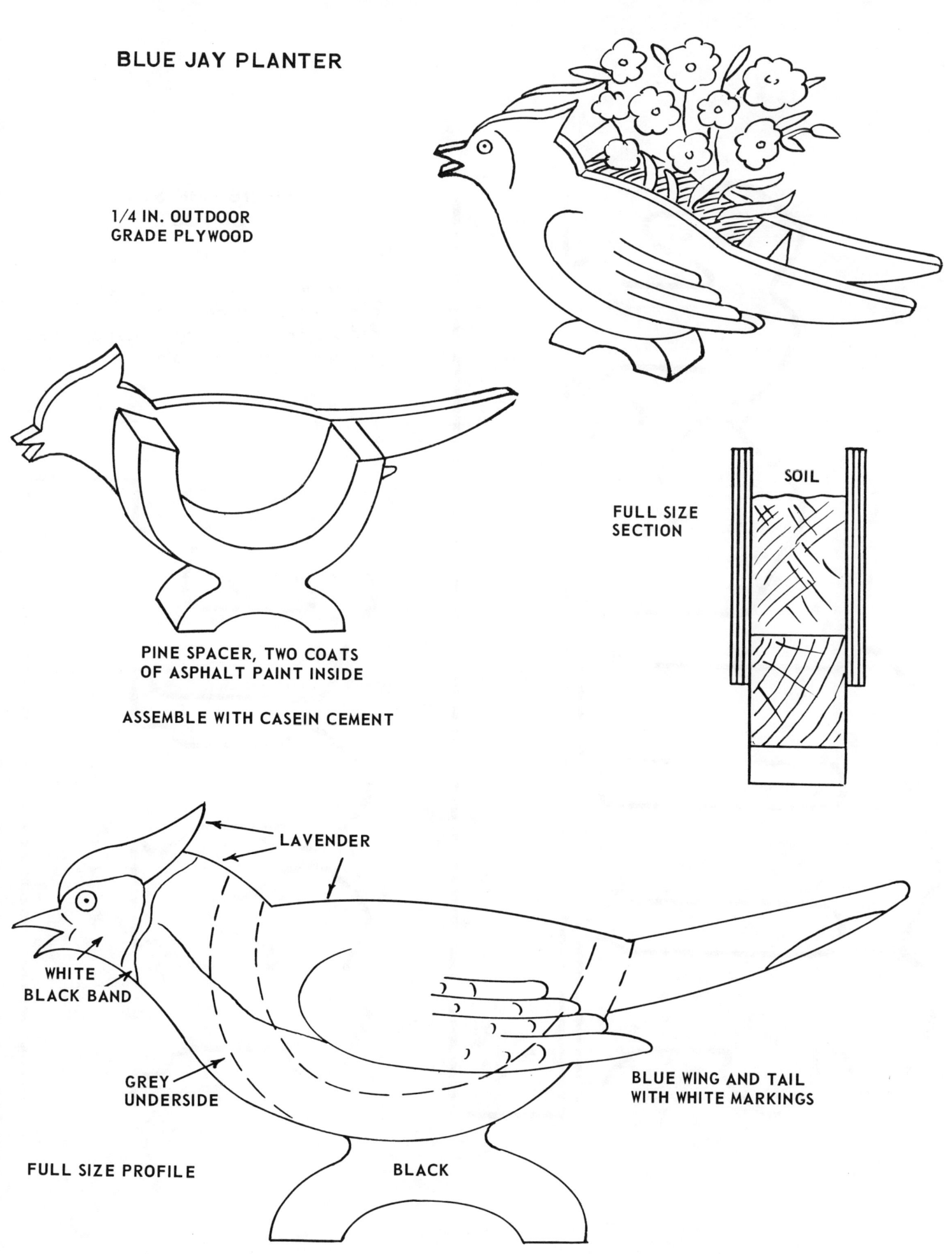

MERRIE CHRISTMAS CUTOUT

Styrofoam, or plywood 1/2 in. thick, is recommended for this neat Holiday decoration. Styrofoam may be colored red or green, by using almost any kind of oil or water base paint.

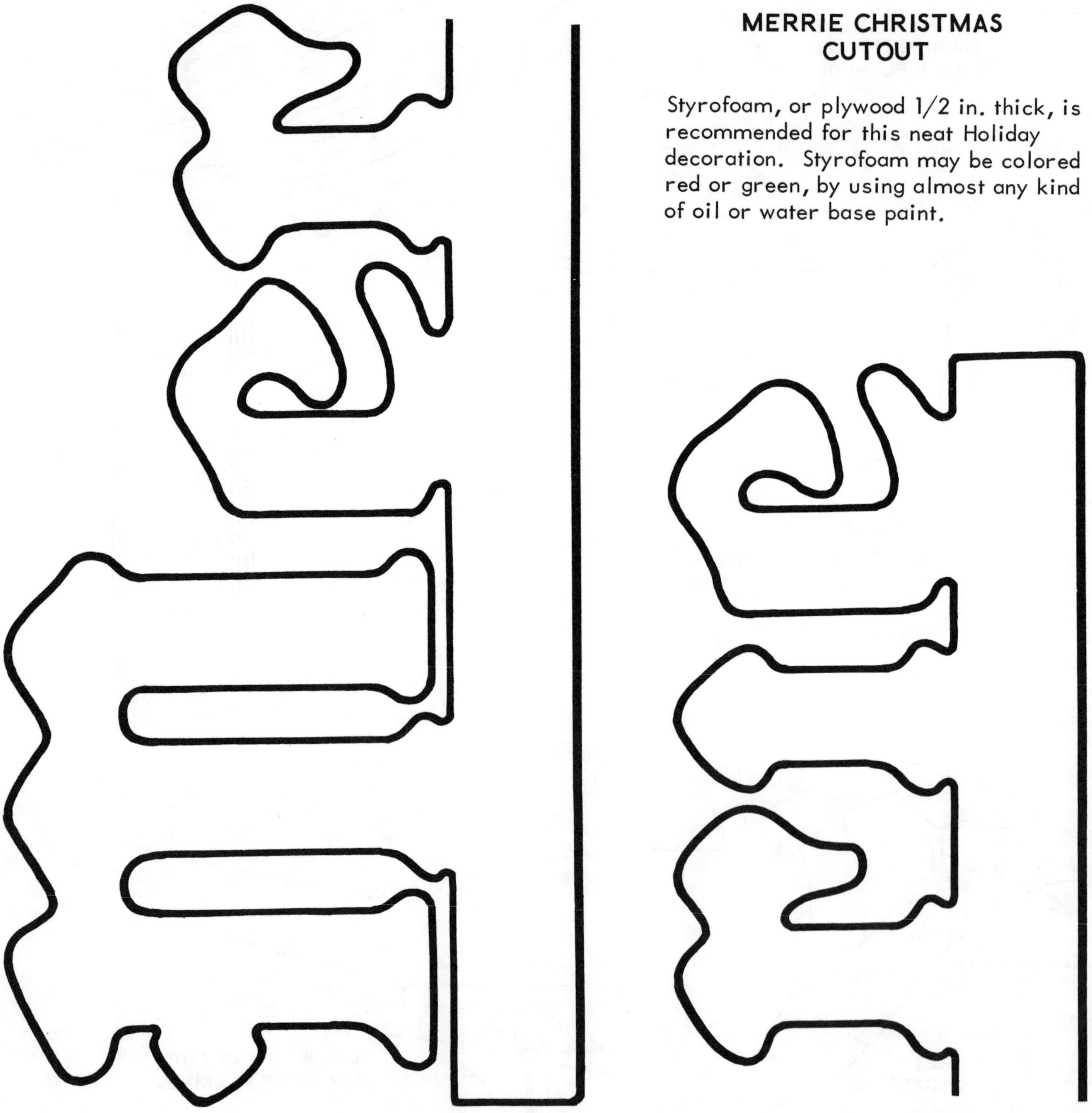

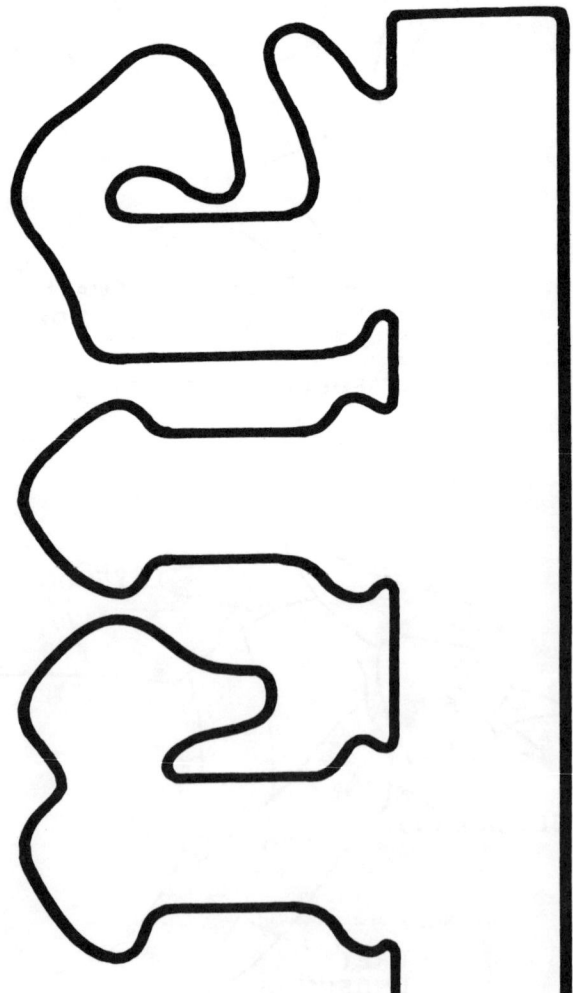

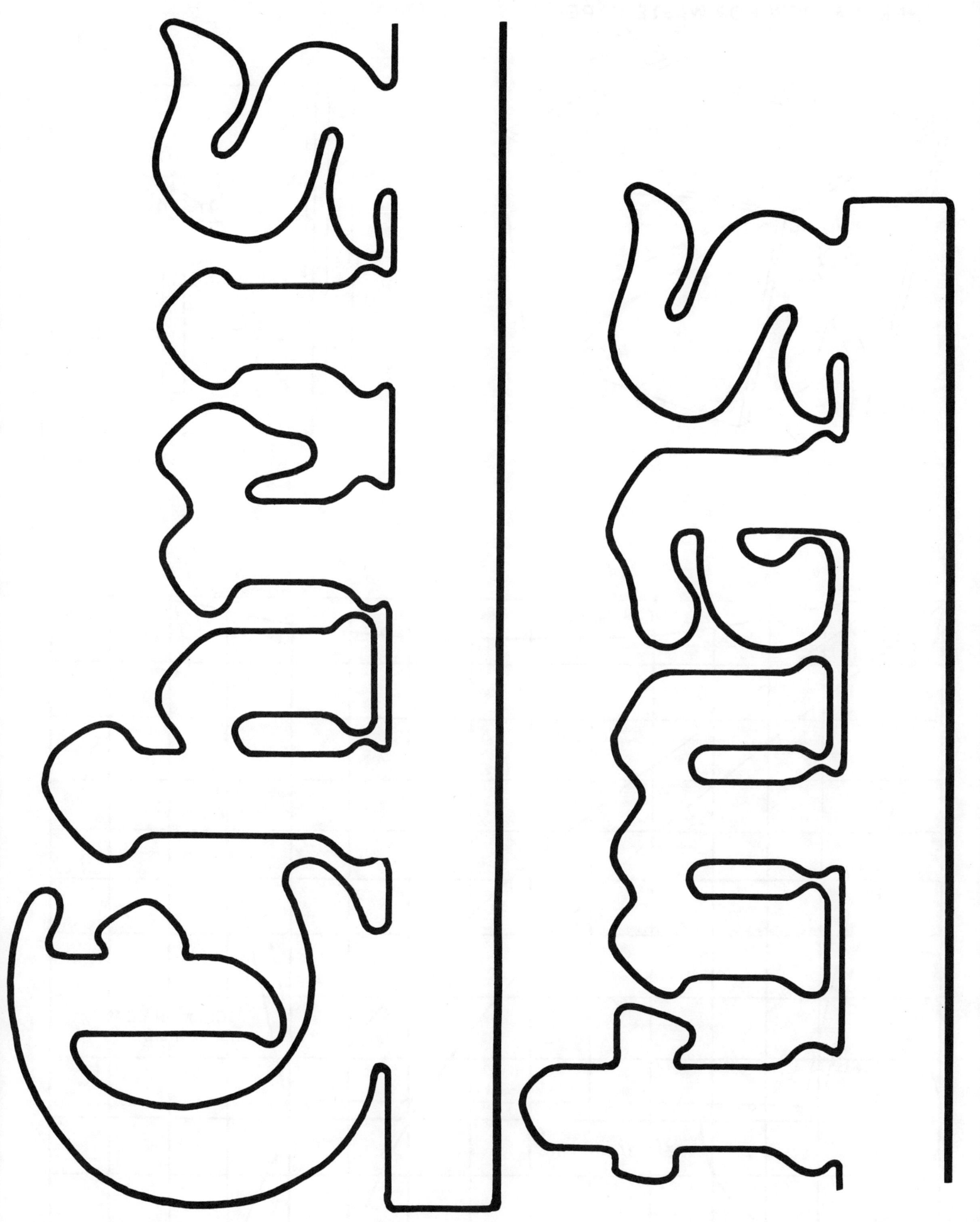

WHEELBARROW FOR WASTE PAPER

11
1/4
9
1/4

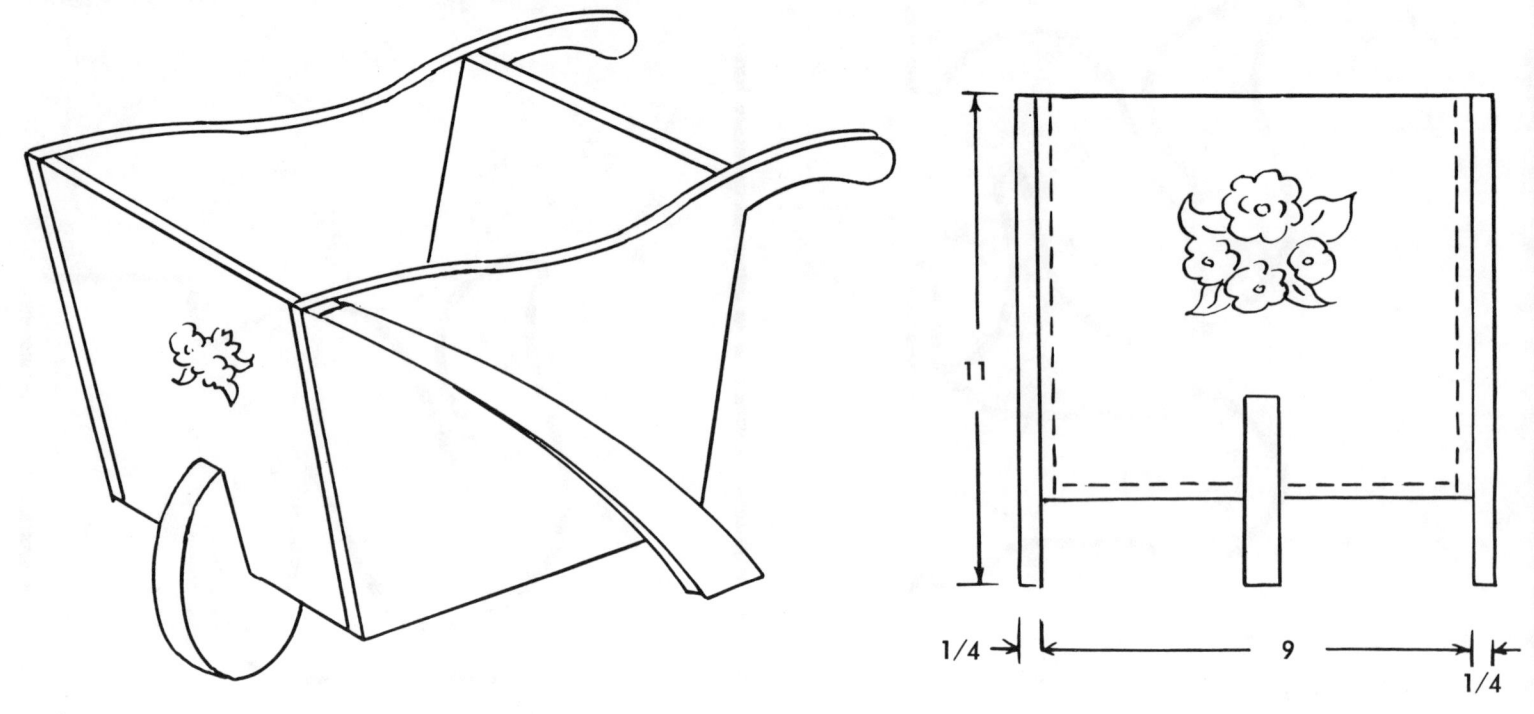

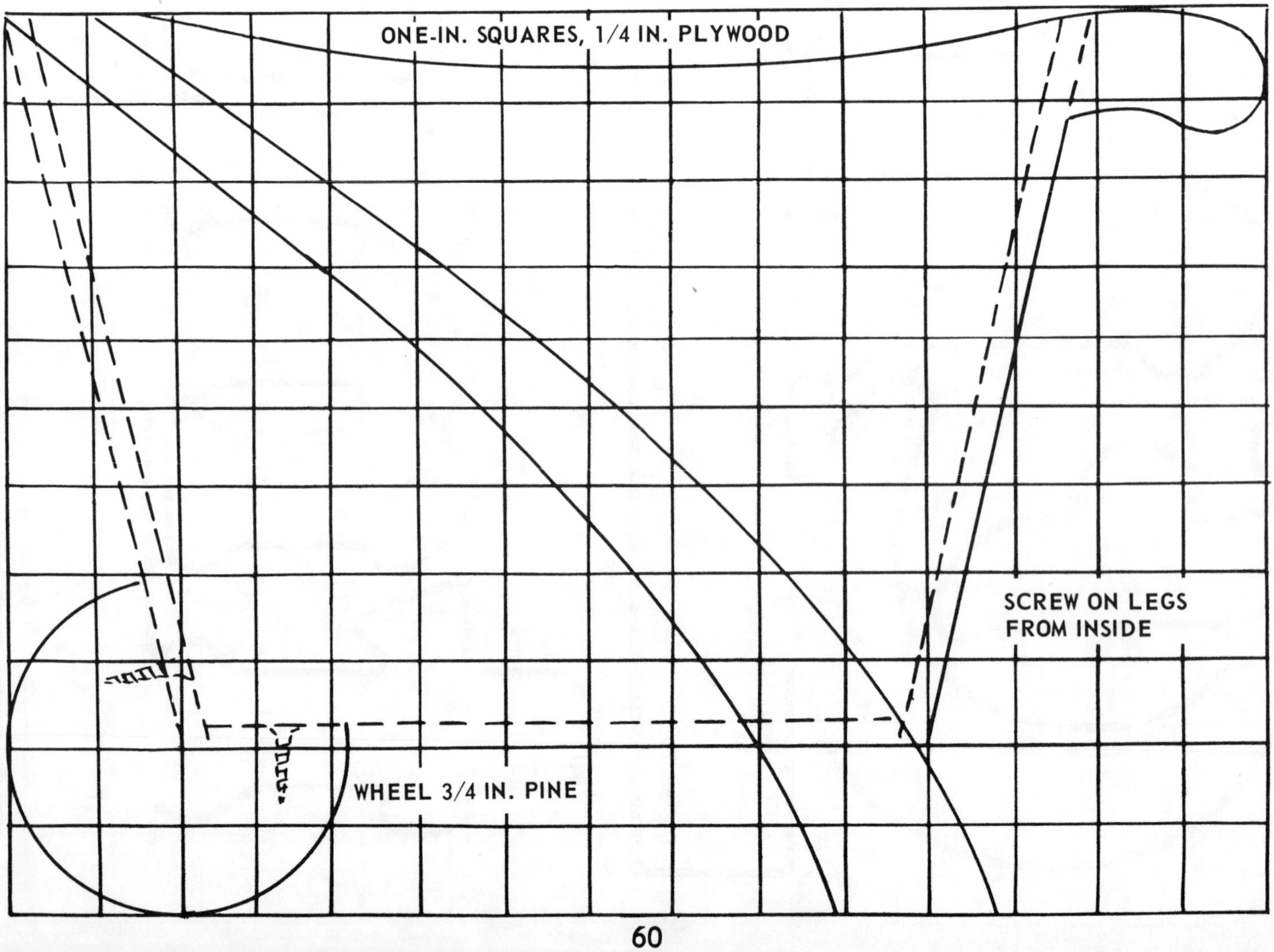

ONE-IN. SQUARES, 1/4 IN. PLYWOOD
SCREW ON LEGS
FROM INSIDE
WHEEL 3/4 IN. PINE

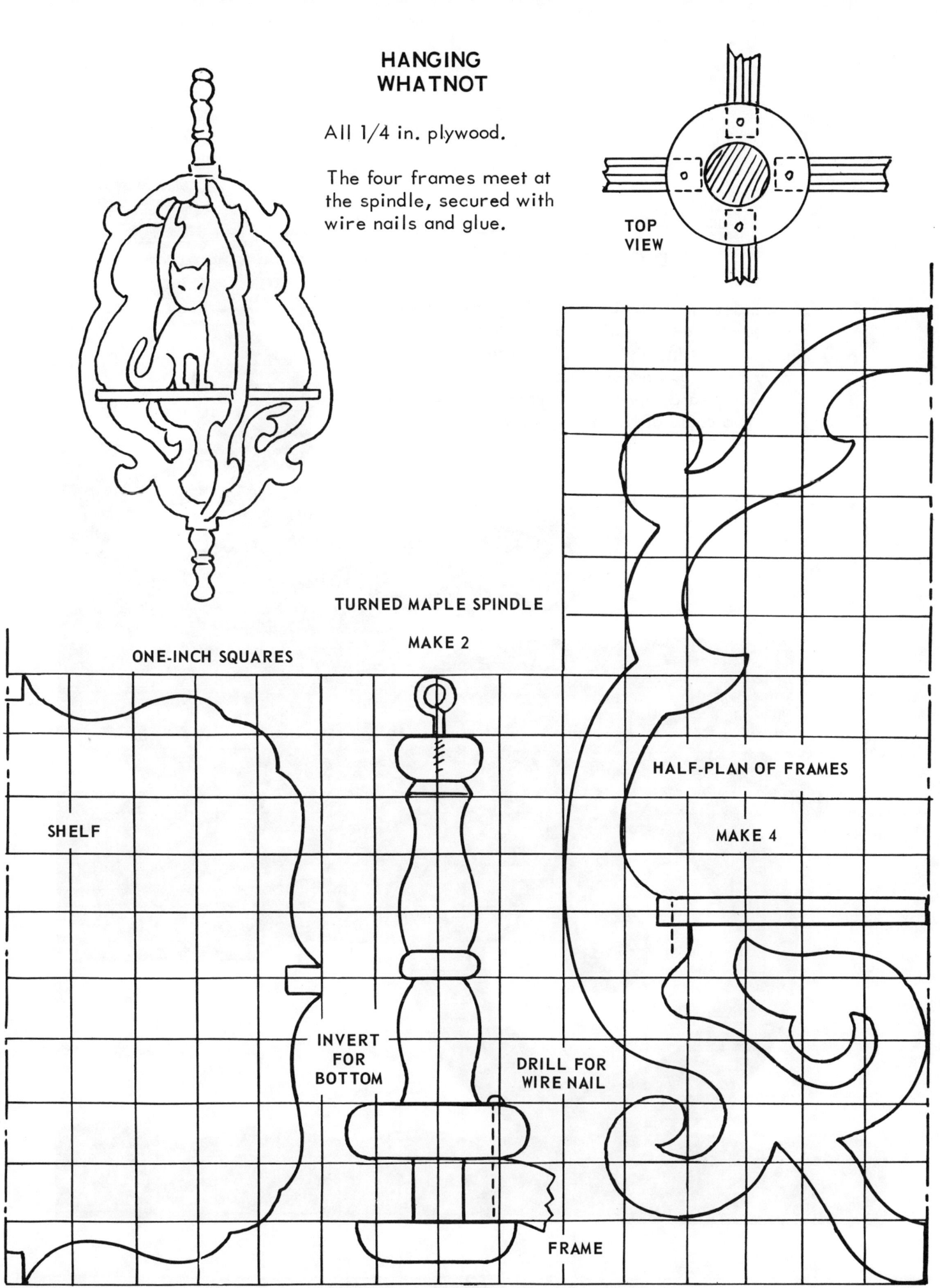

OLD CAR PLAQUE

This design works up into a very attractive plaque for a recreation room, den, hall, or porch. 1/4 in. plywood or pressed wood may be used -- pressed wood is preferable. Saw out, sand, give wood a coat of shellac and two coats of flat black paint.

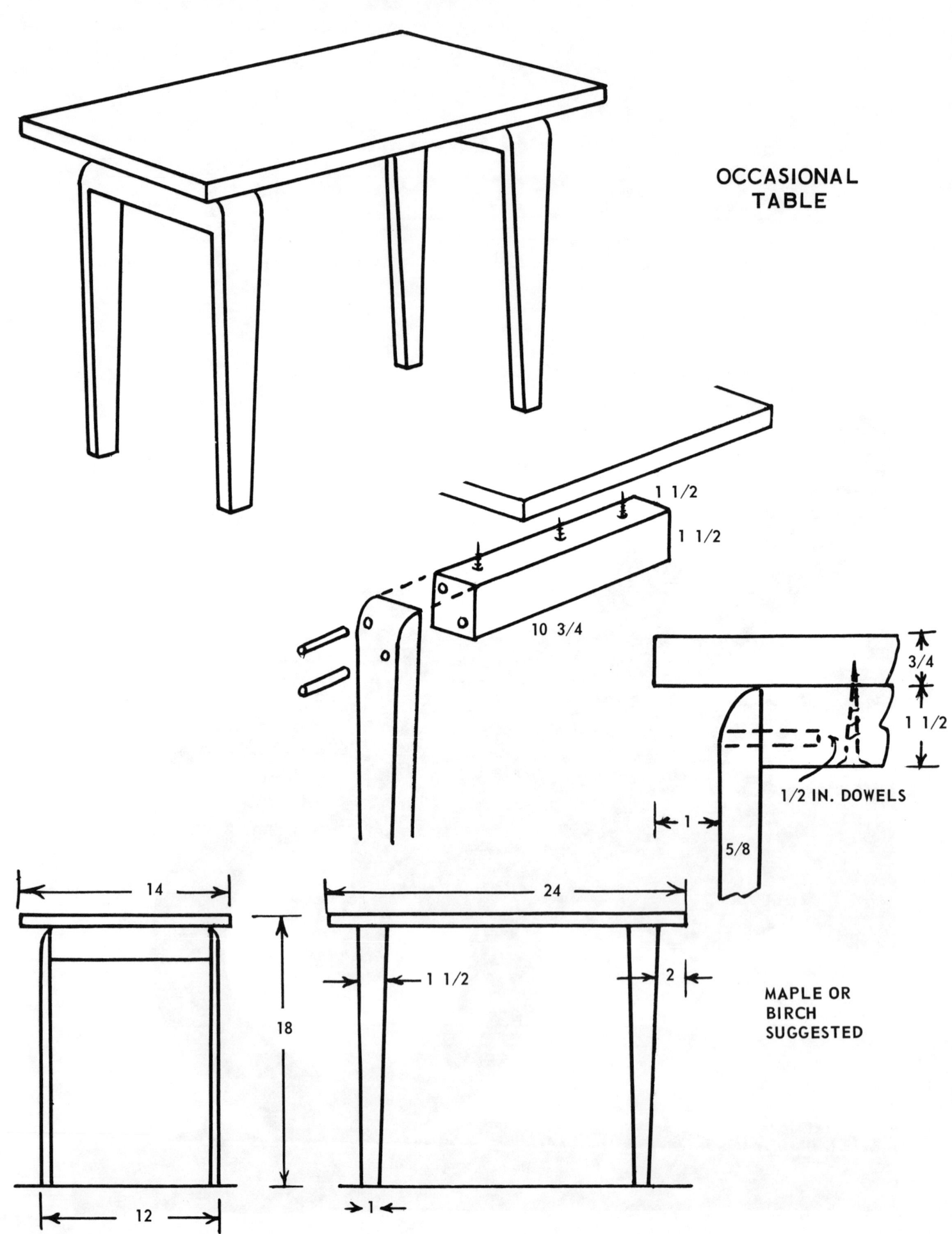

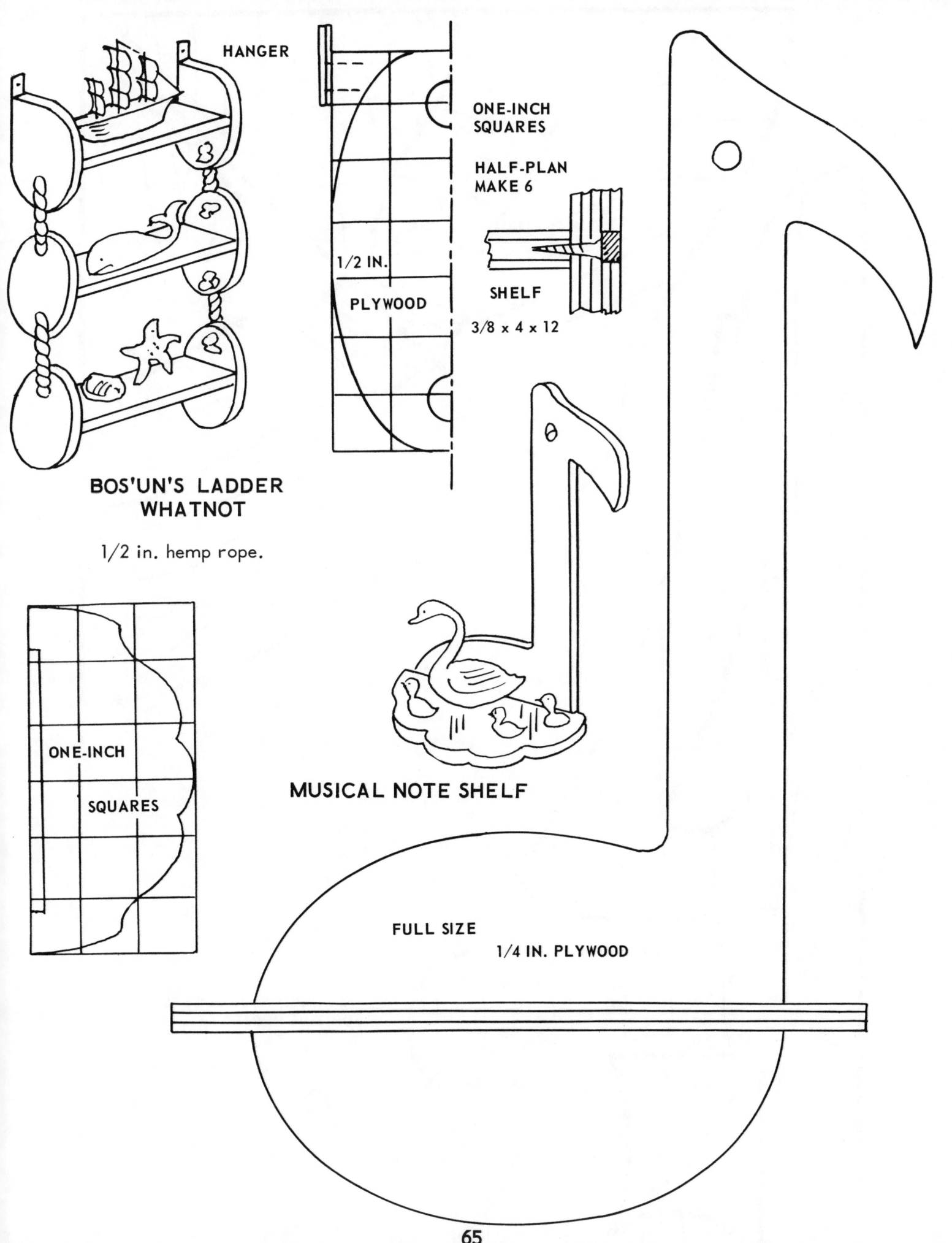

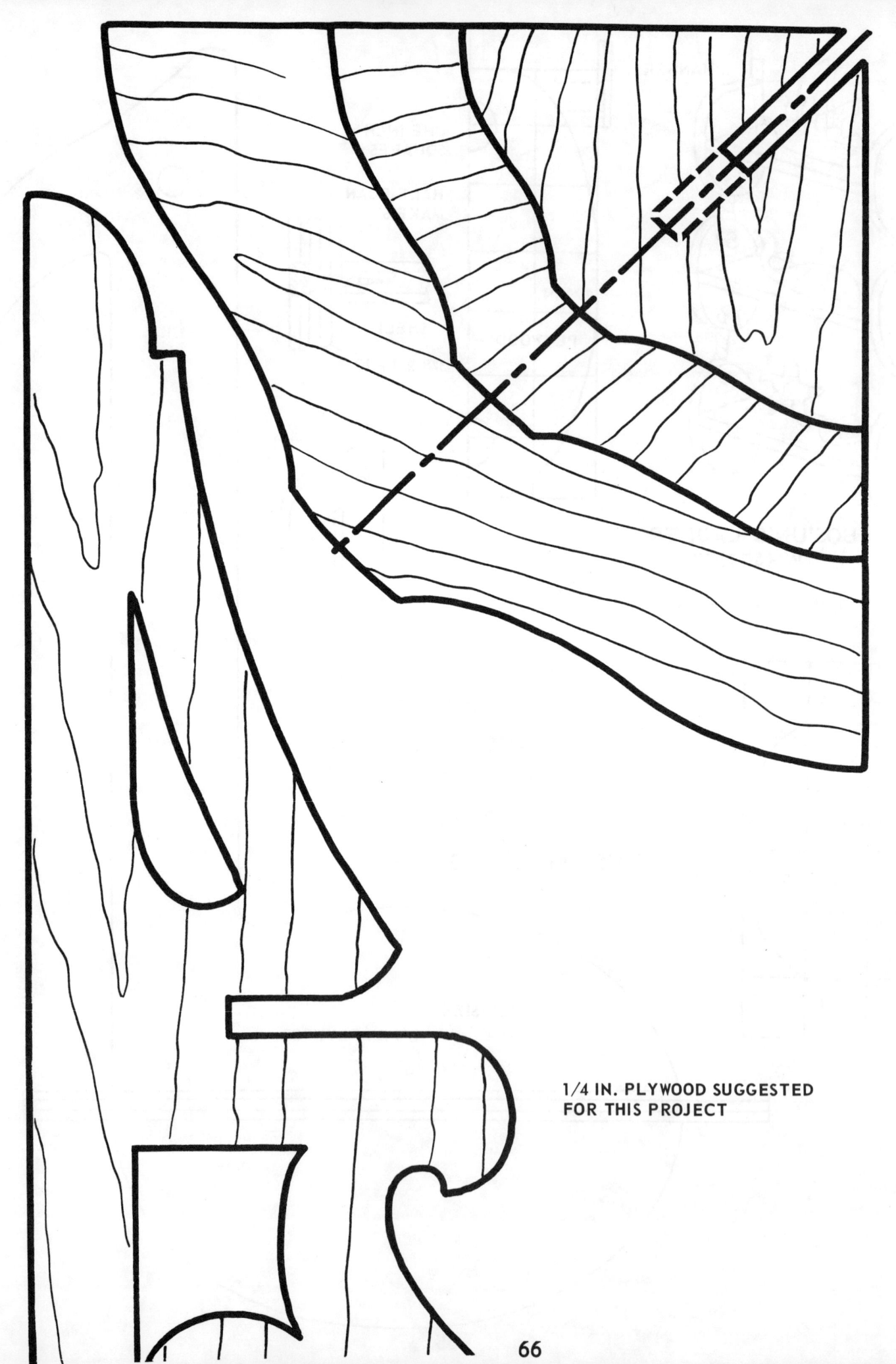

1/4 IN. PLYWOOD SUGGESTED FOR THIS PROJECT

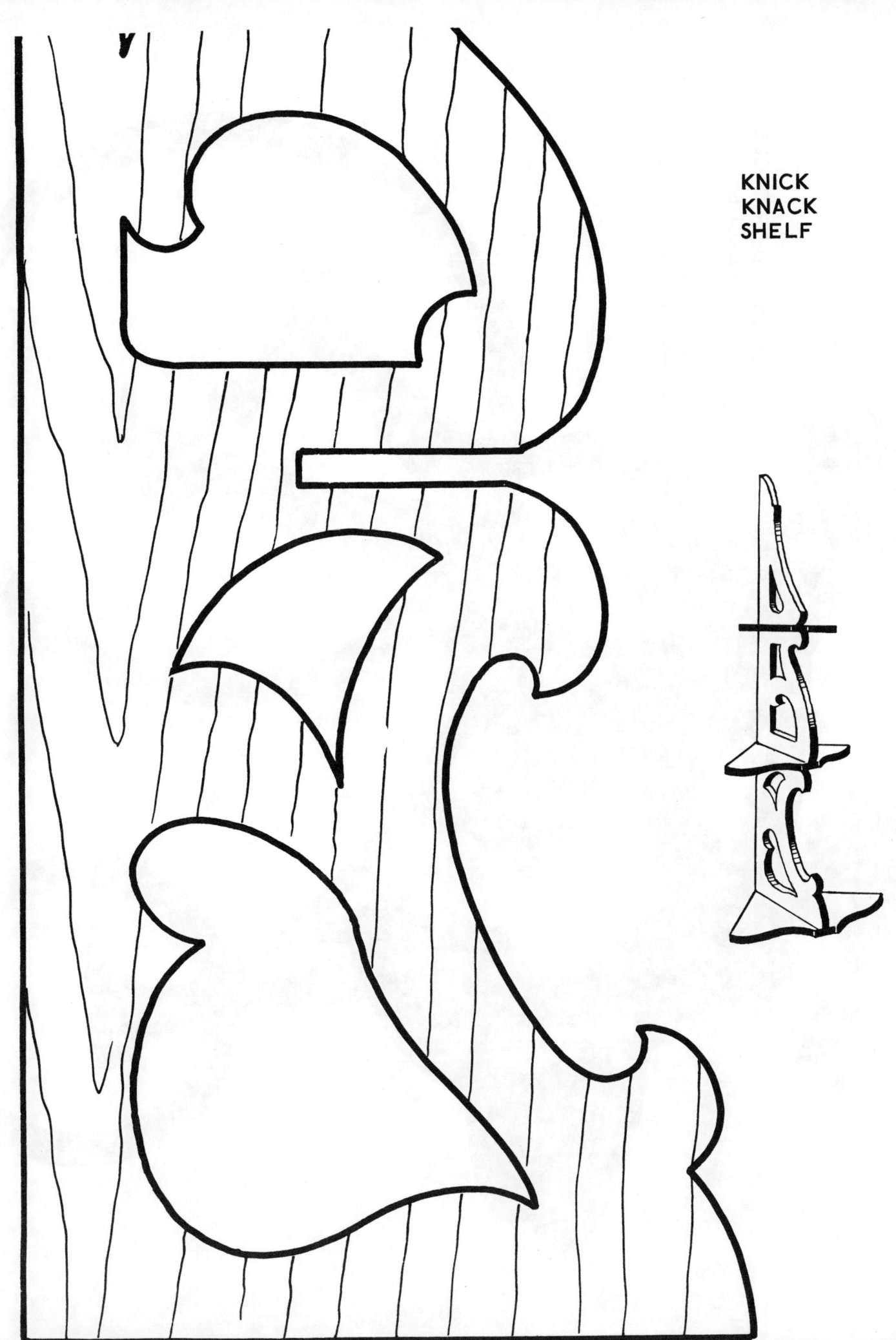

KNICK KNACK SHELF

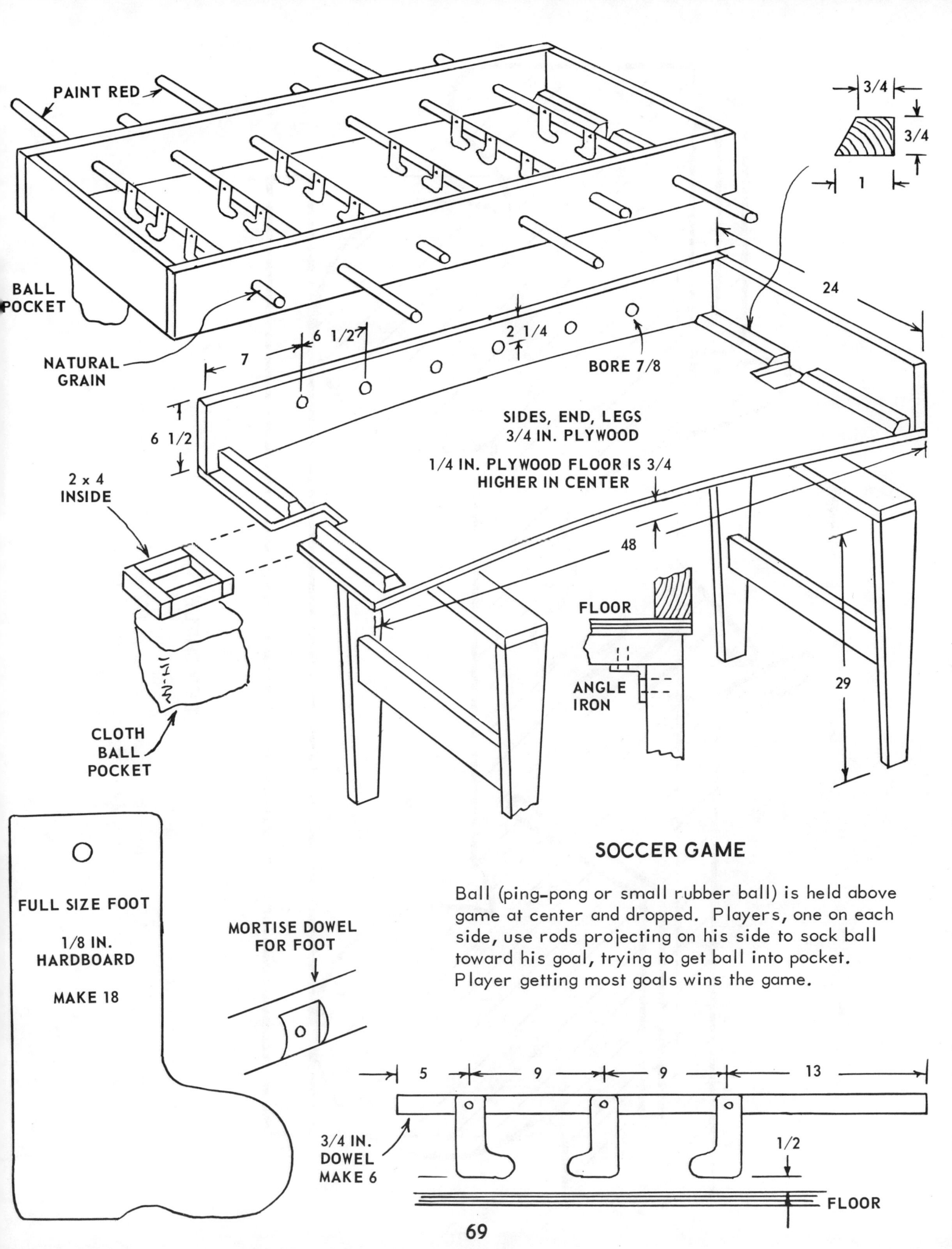

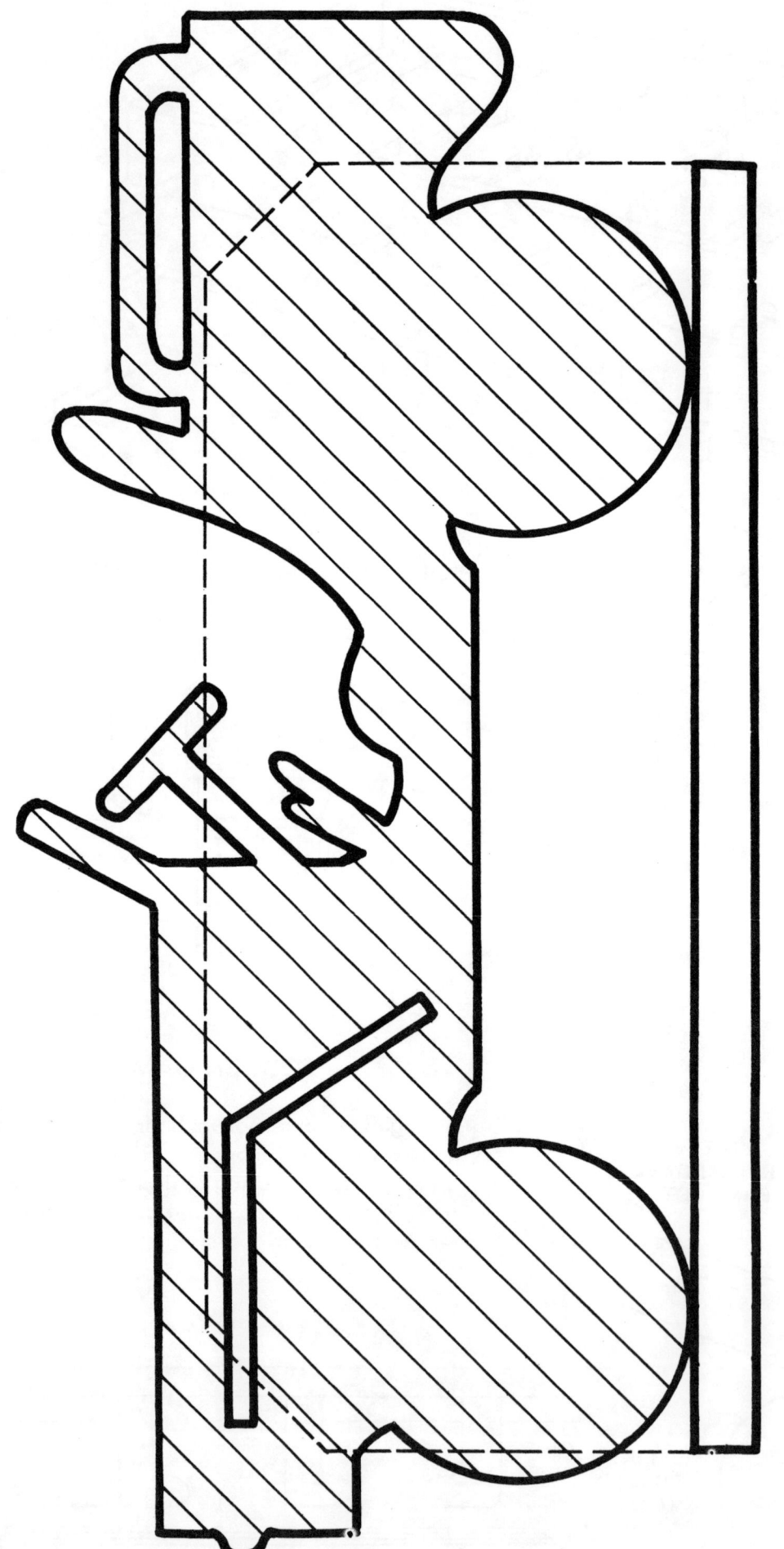

JEEP SHELF

1/4 in. plywood suggested for jeep, 1/2 in. for shelf. Shelf size is indicated by dotted line. Finish with enamel.

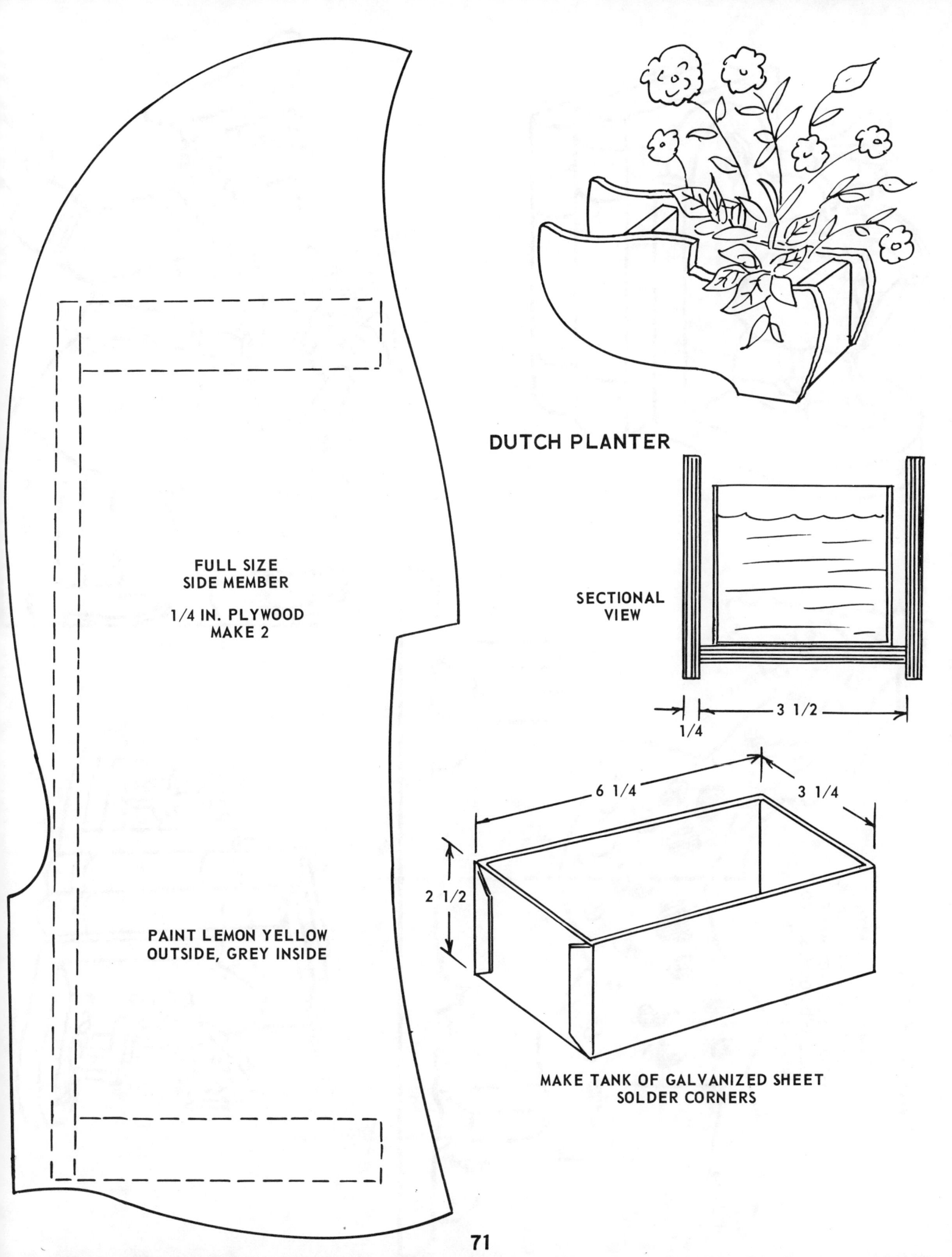

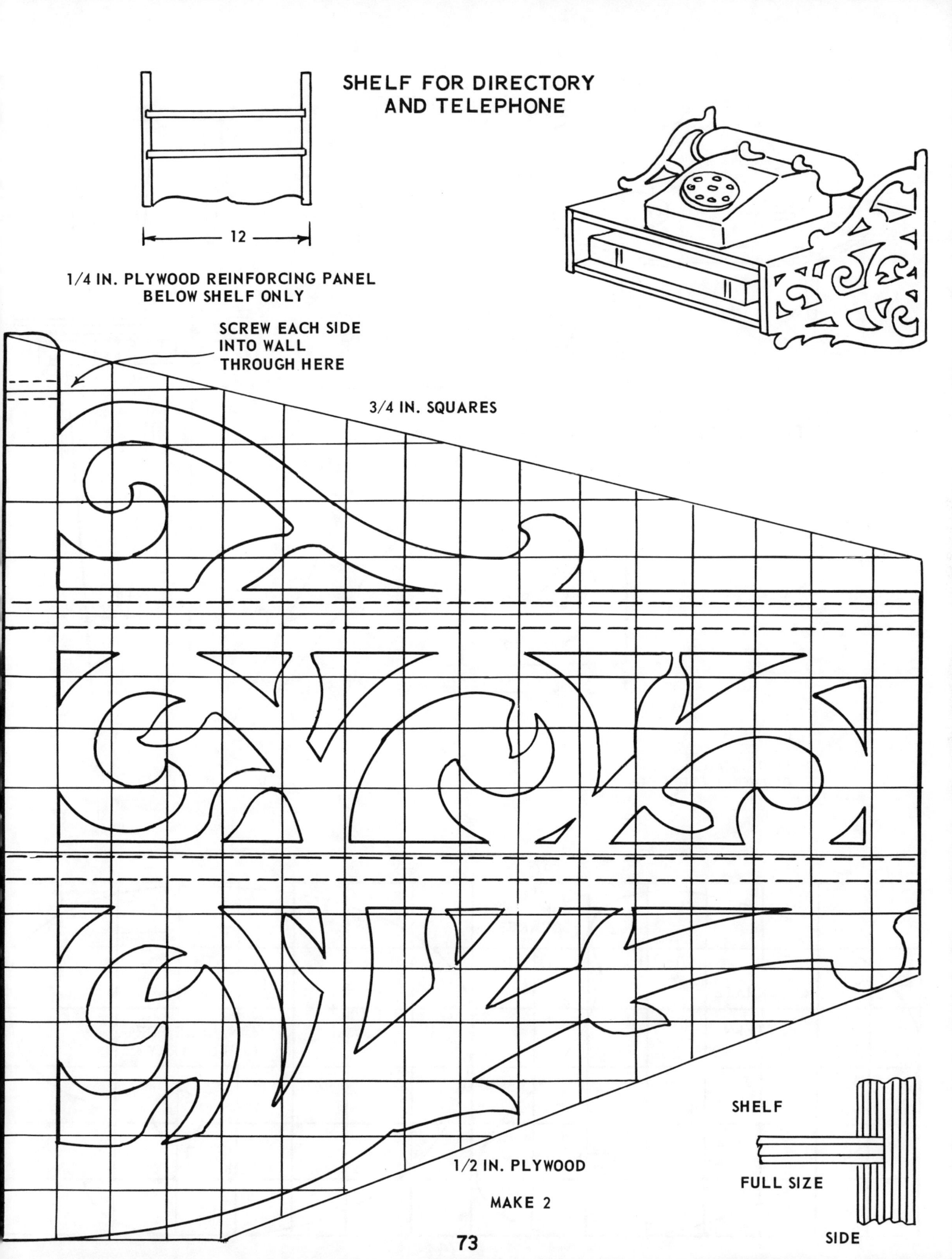

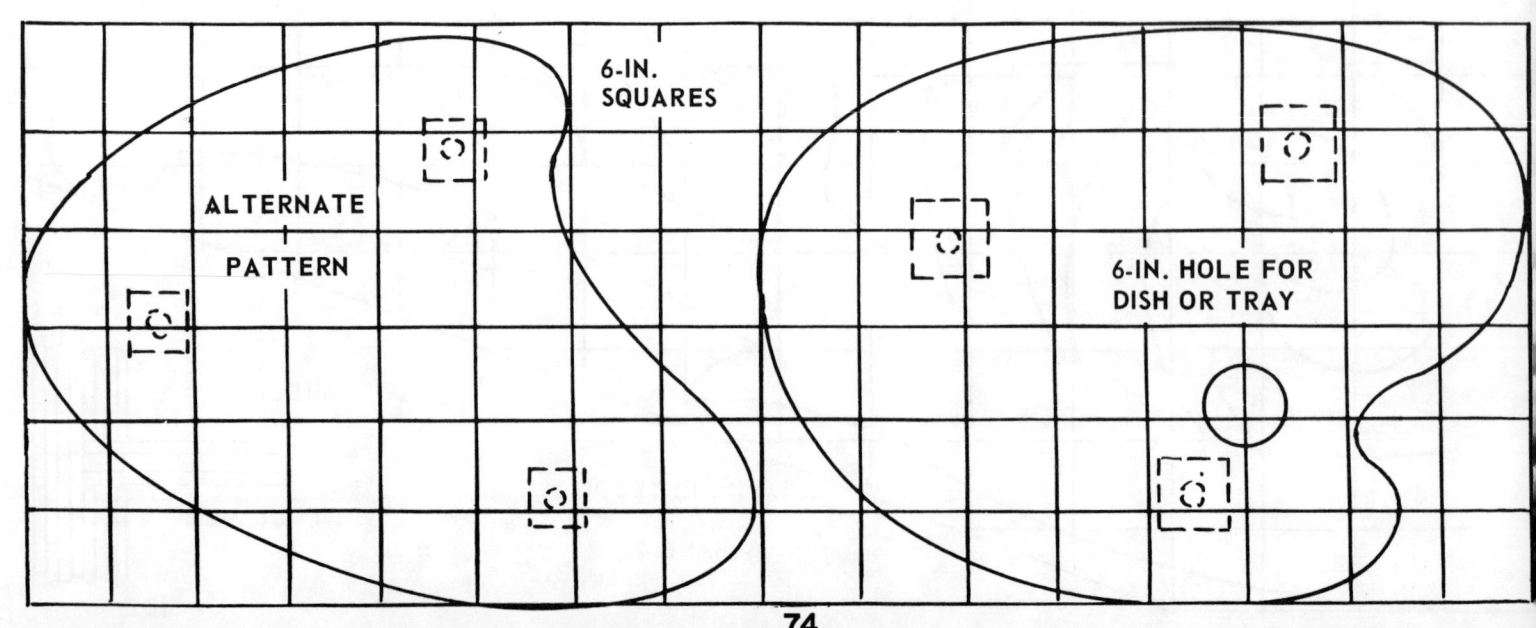

ARTIST'S COFFEE TABLE

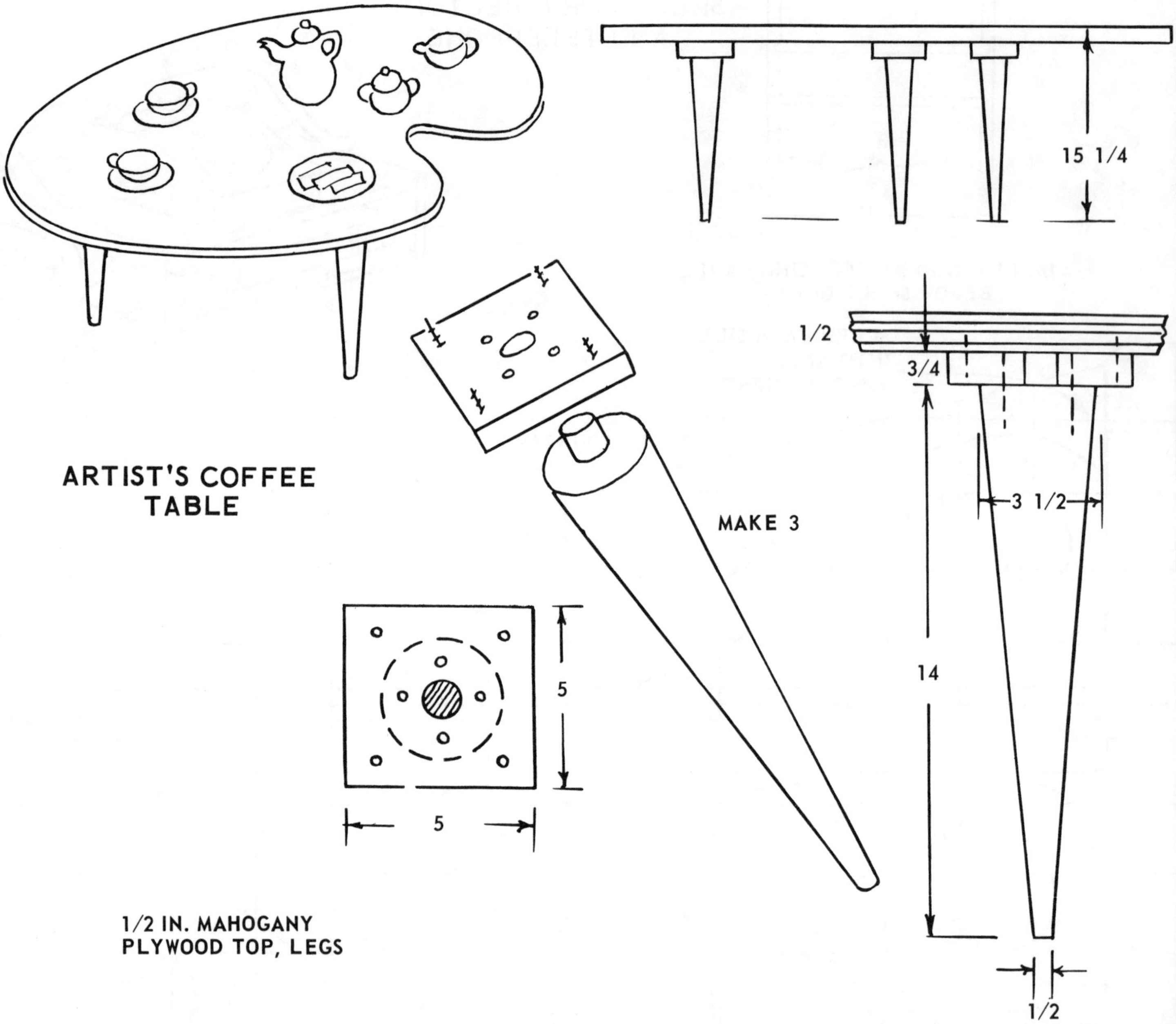

MAKE 3

1/2 IN. MAHOGANY PLYWOOD TOP, LEGS

15 1/4
1/2
3/4
3 1/2
14
1/2
5
5

6-IN. SQUARES

ALTERNATE PATTERN

6-IN. HOLE FOR DISH OR TRAY

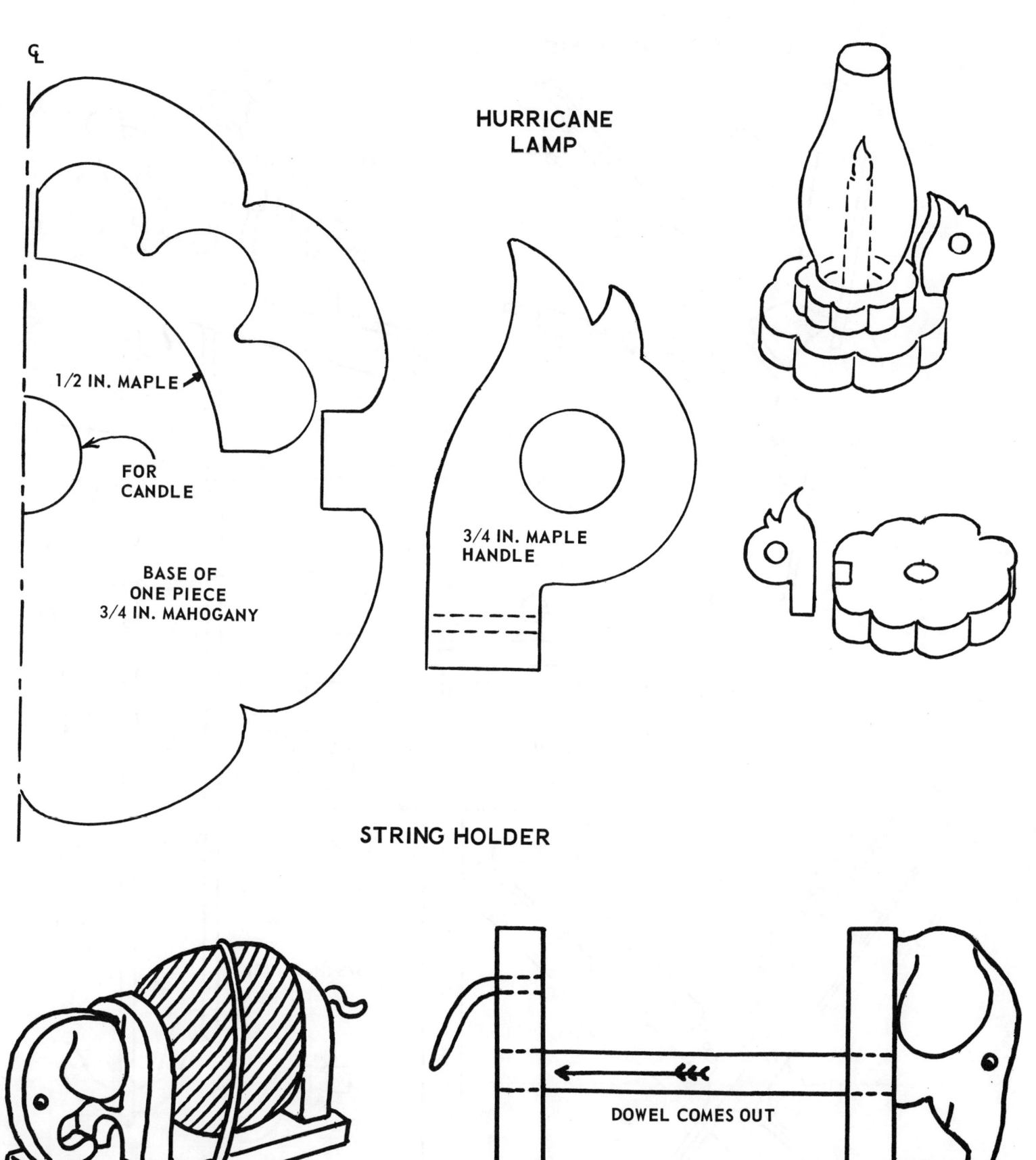

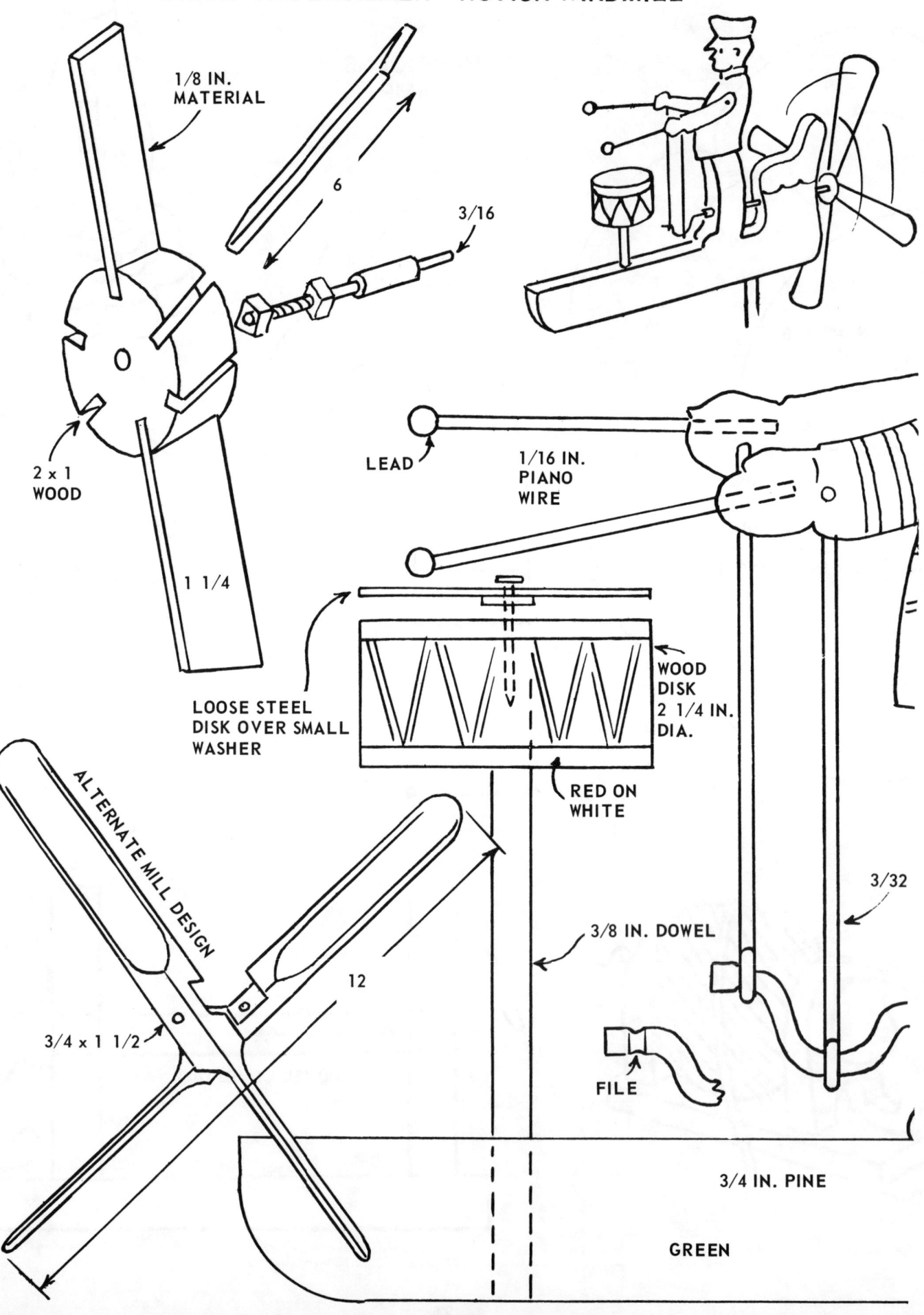

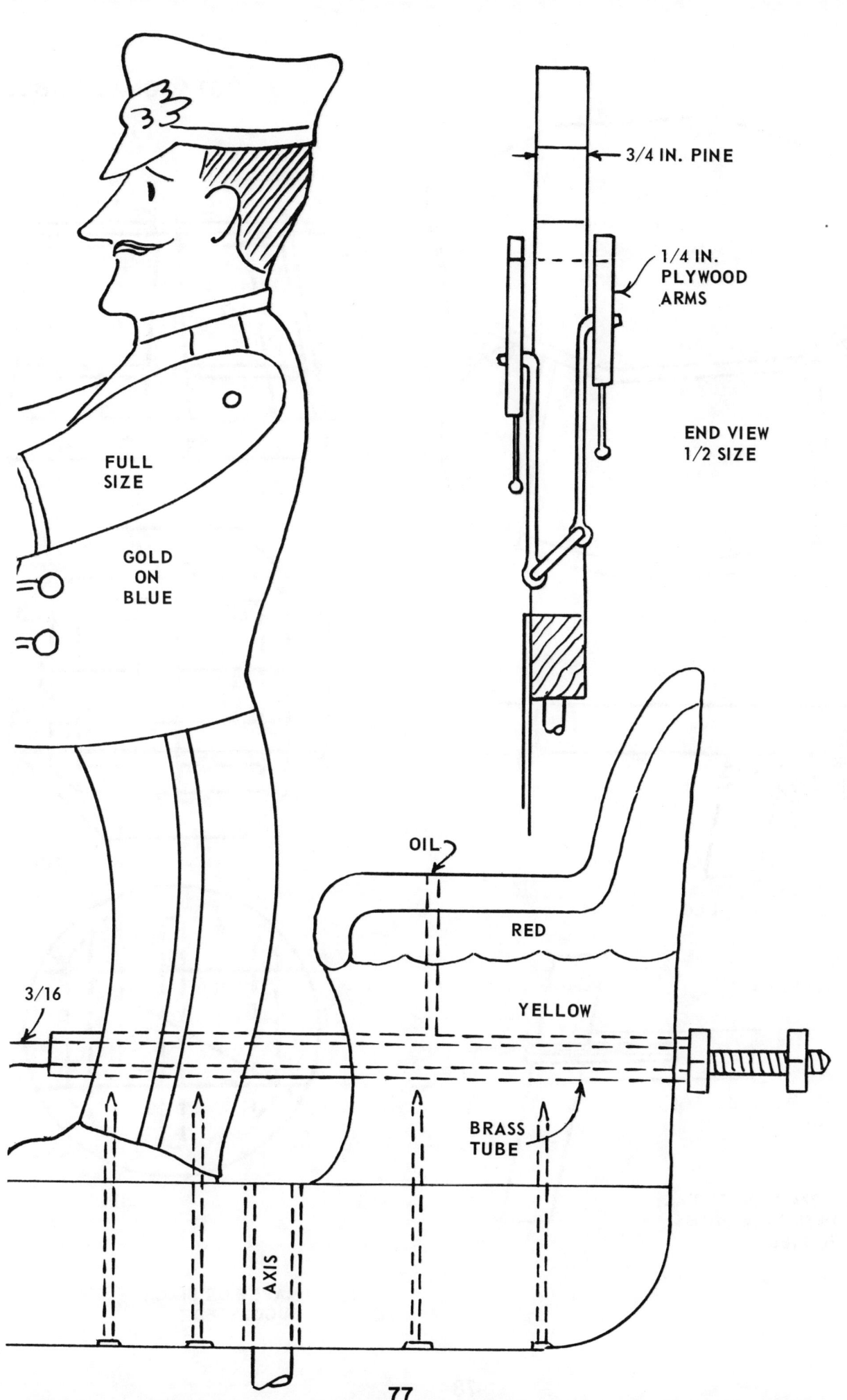

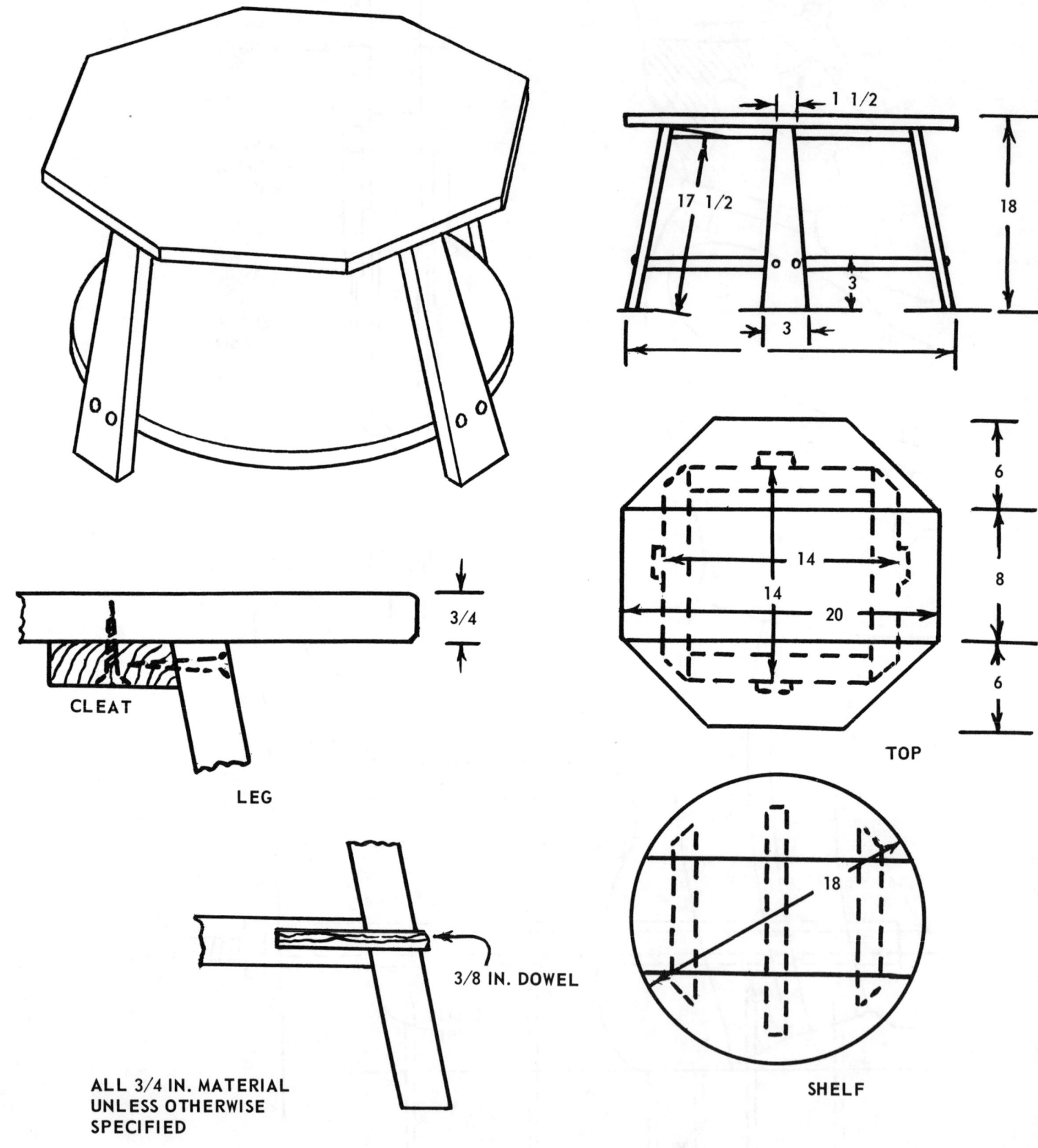

SILENT BUTLER

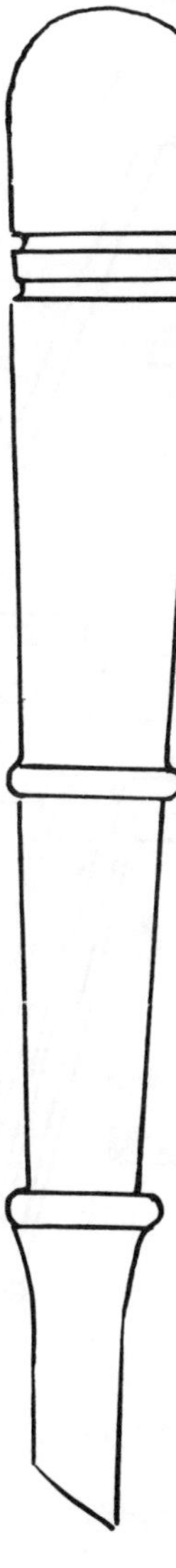

FULL SIZE BIRCH

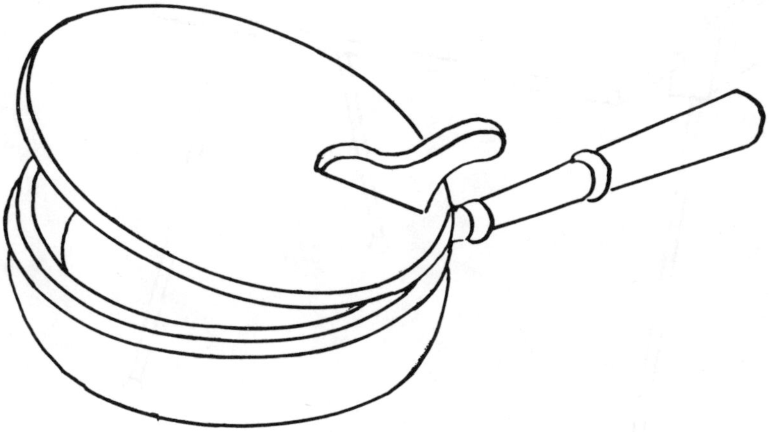

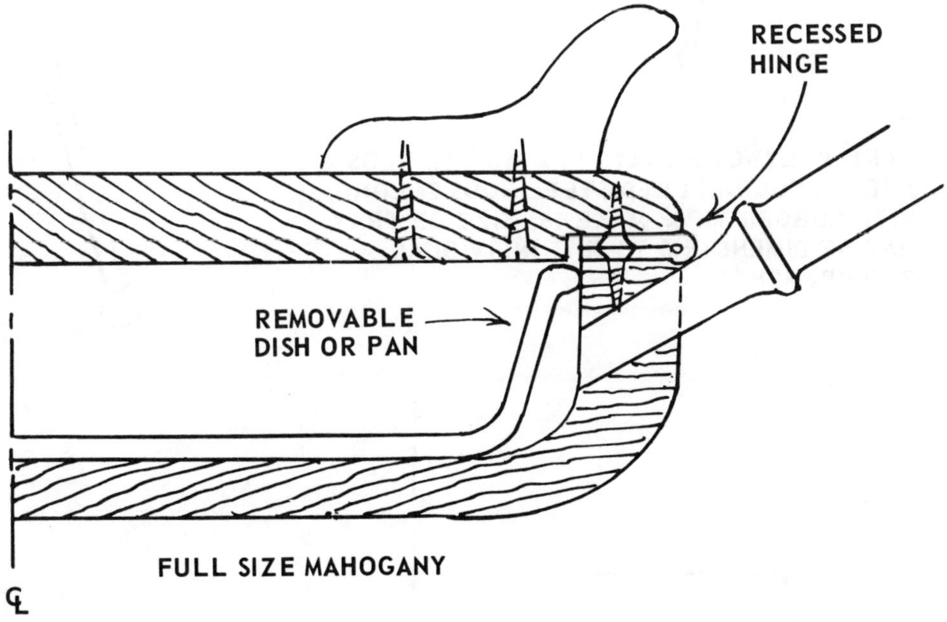

RECESSED HINGE

REMOVABLE DISH OR PAN

FULL SIZE MAHOGANY

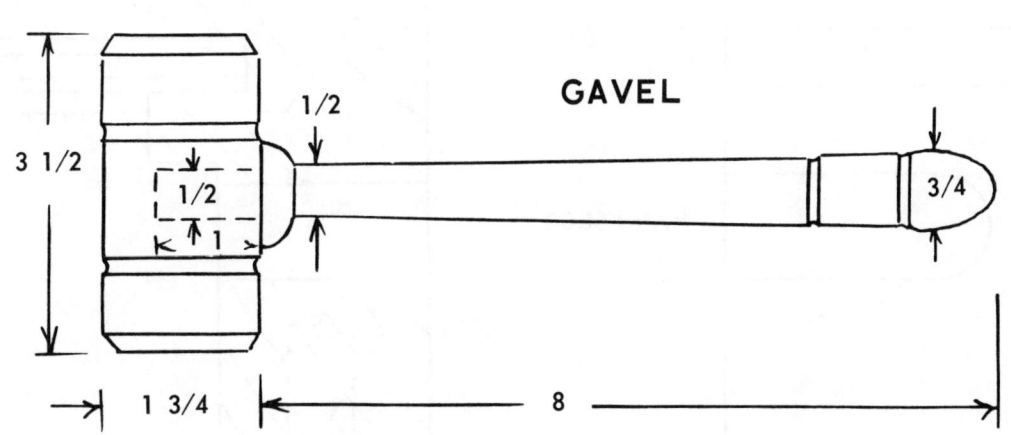

GAVEL

3 1/2
1/2
1/2
1
1 3/4
3/4
8

NESTED TV TABLES

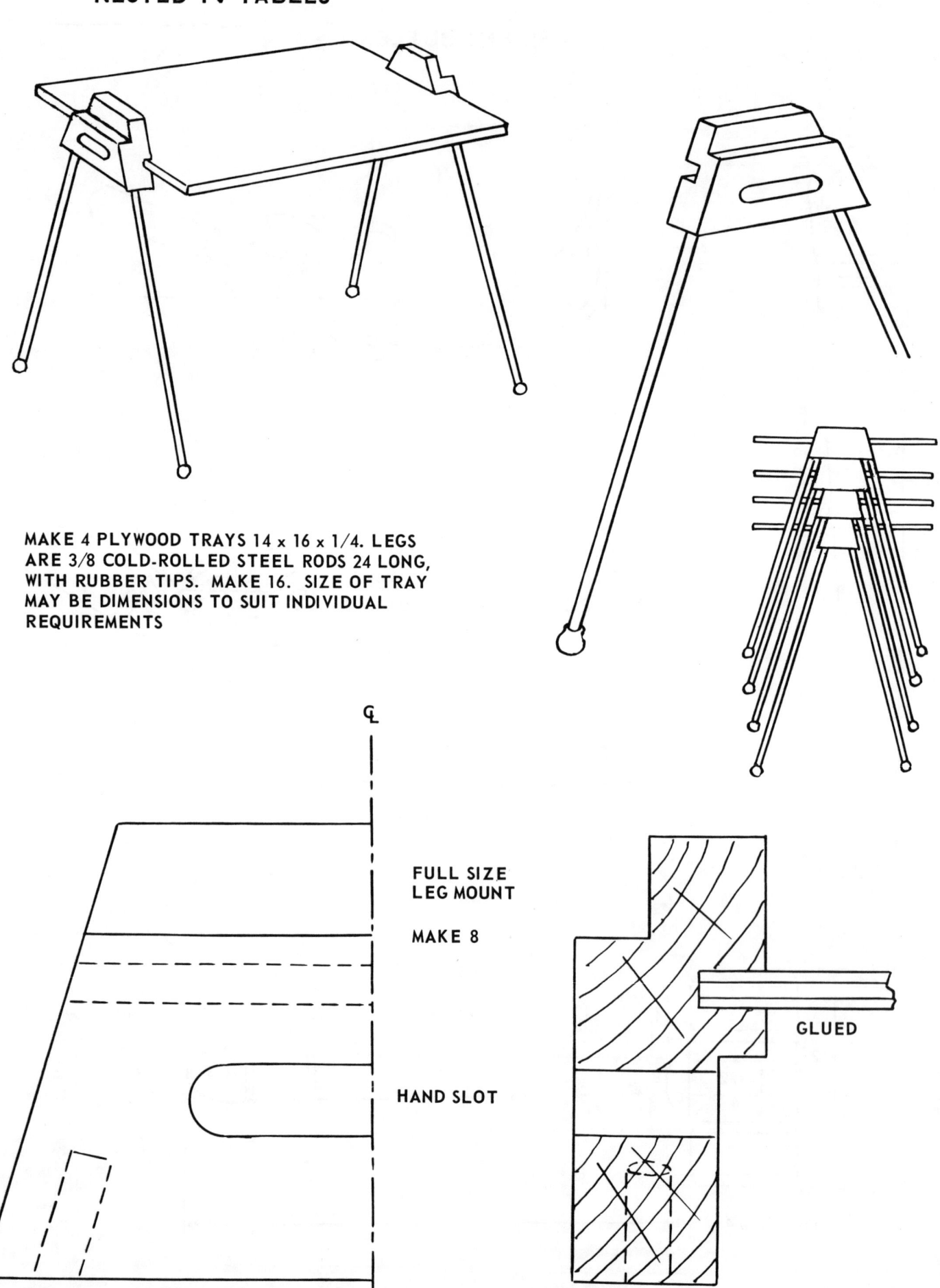

MAKE 4 PLYWOOD TRAYS 14 x 16 x 1/4. LEGS ARE 3/8 COLD-ROLLED STEEL RODS 24 LONG, WITH RUBBER TIPS. MAKE 16. SIZE OF TRAY MAY BE DIMENSIONS TO SUIT INDIVIDUAL REQUIREMENTS

FULL SIZE LEG MOUNT

MAKE 8

HAND SLOT

GLUED

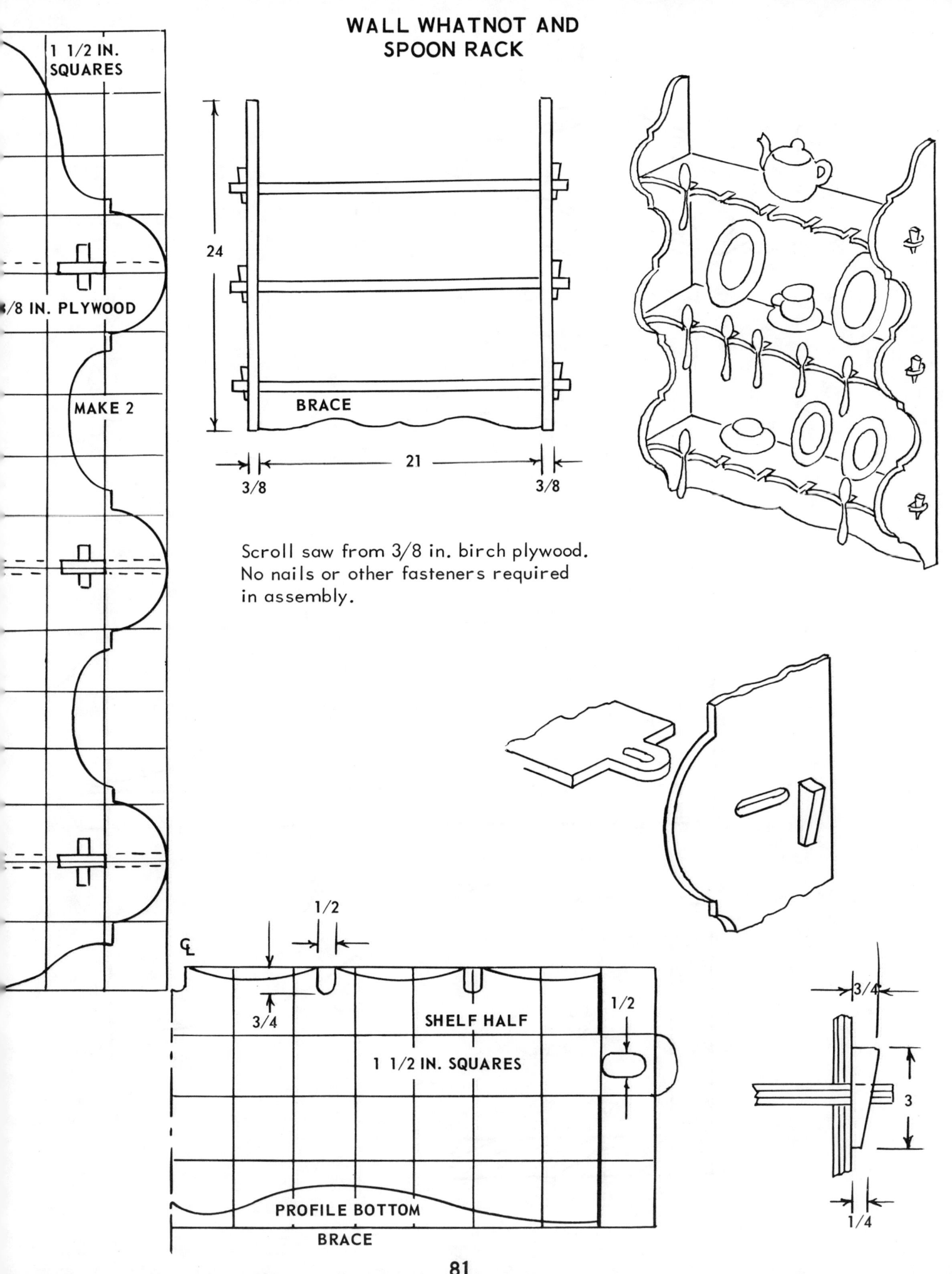

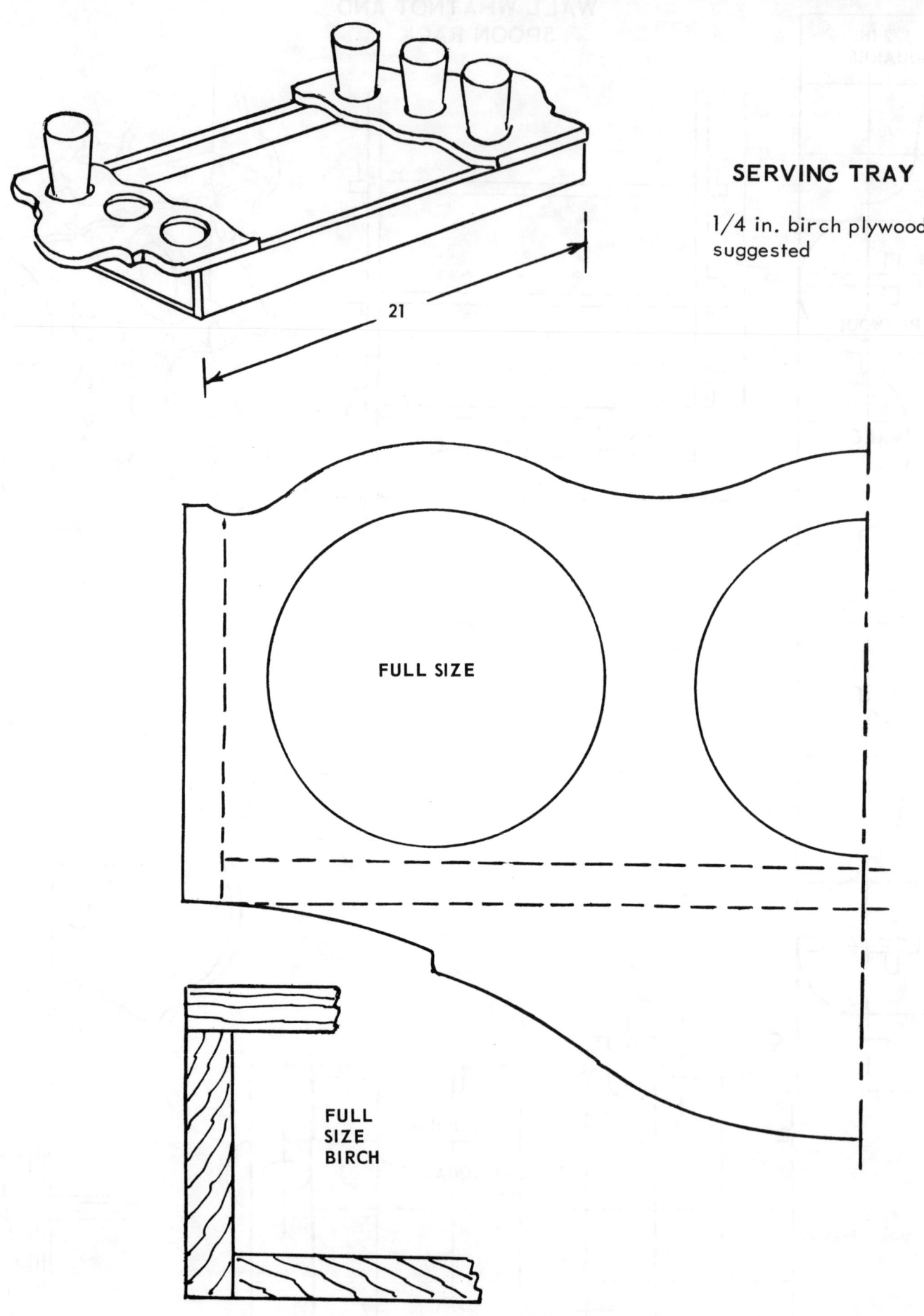

SERVING TRAY

1/4 in. birch plywood suggested

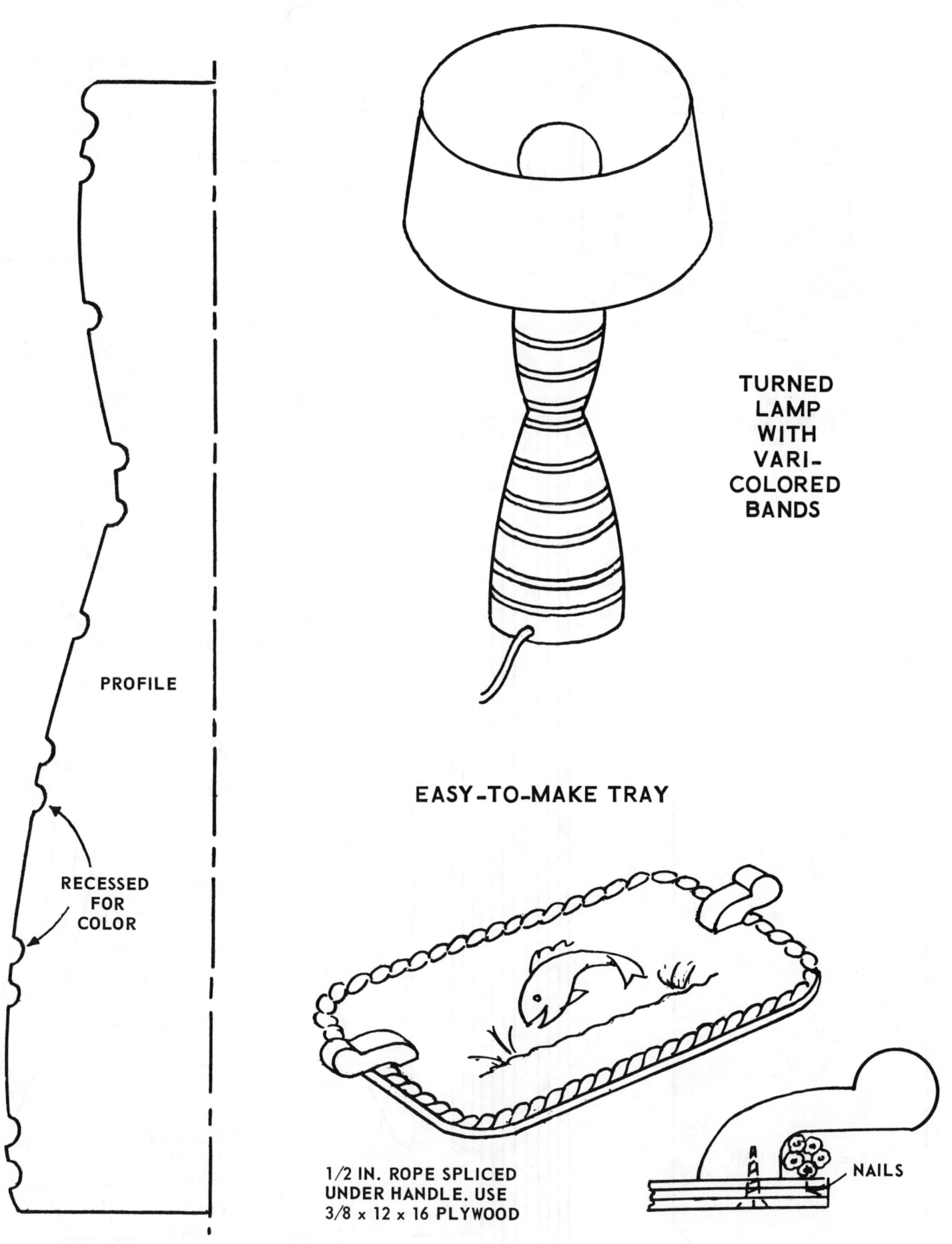

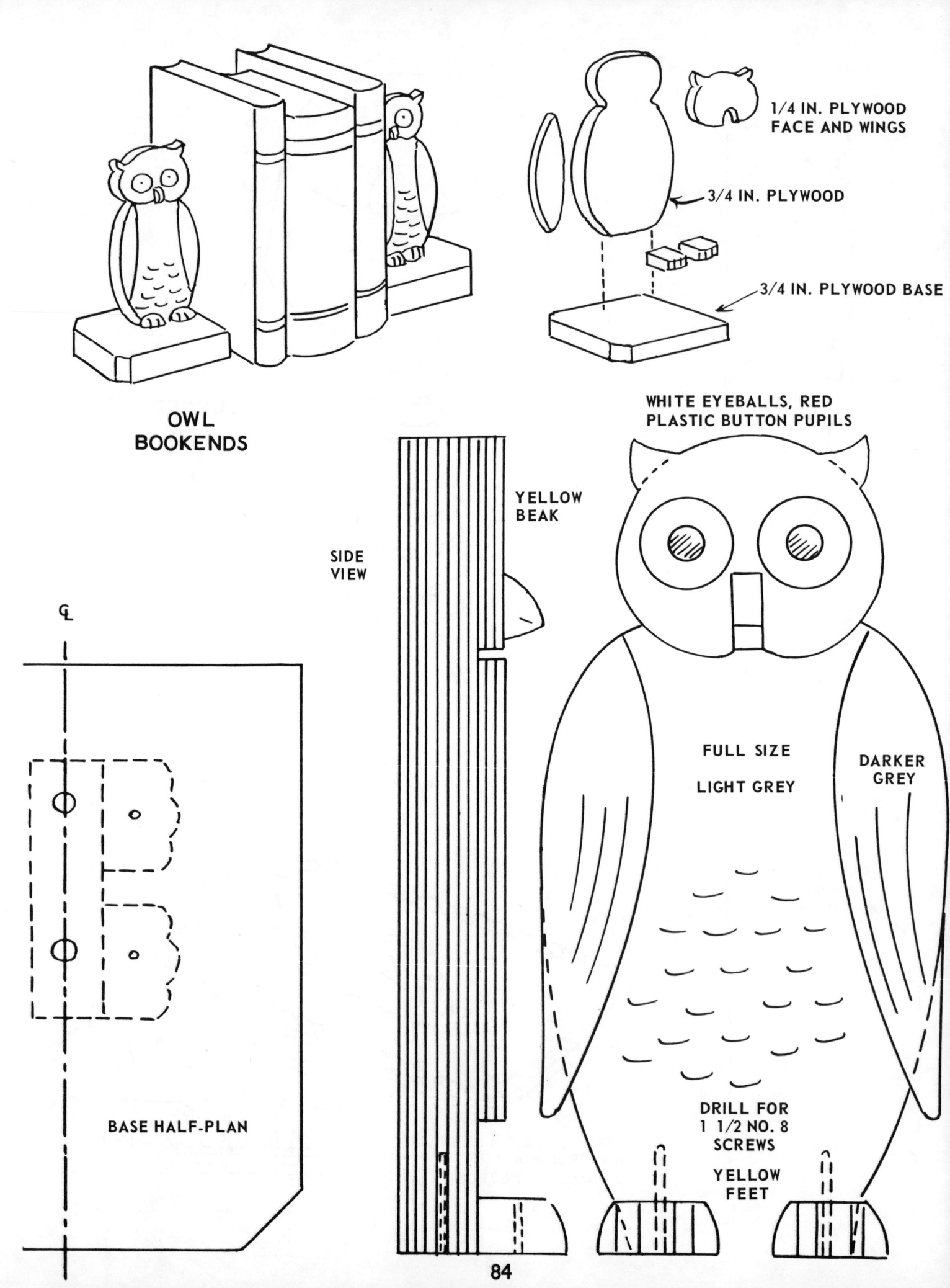

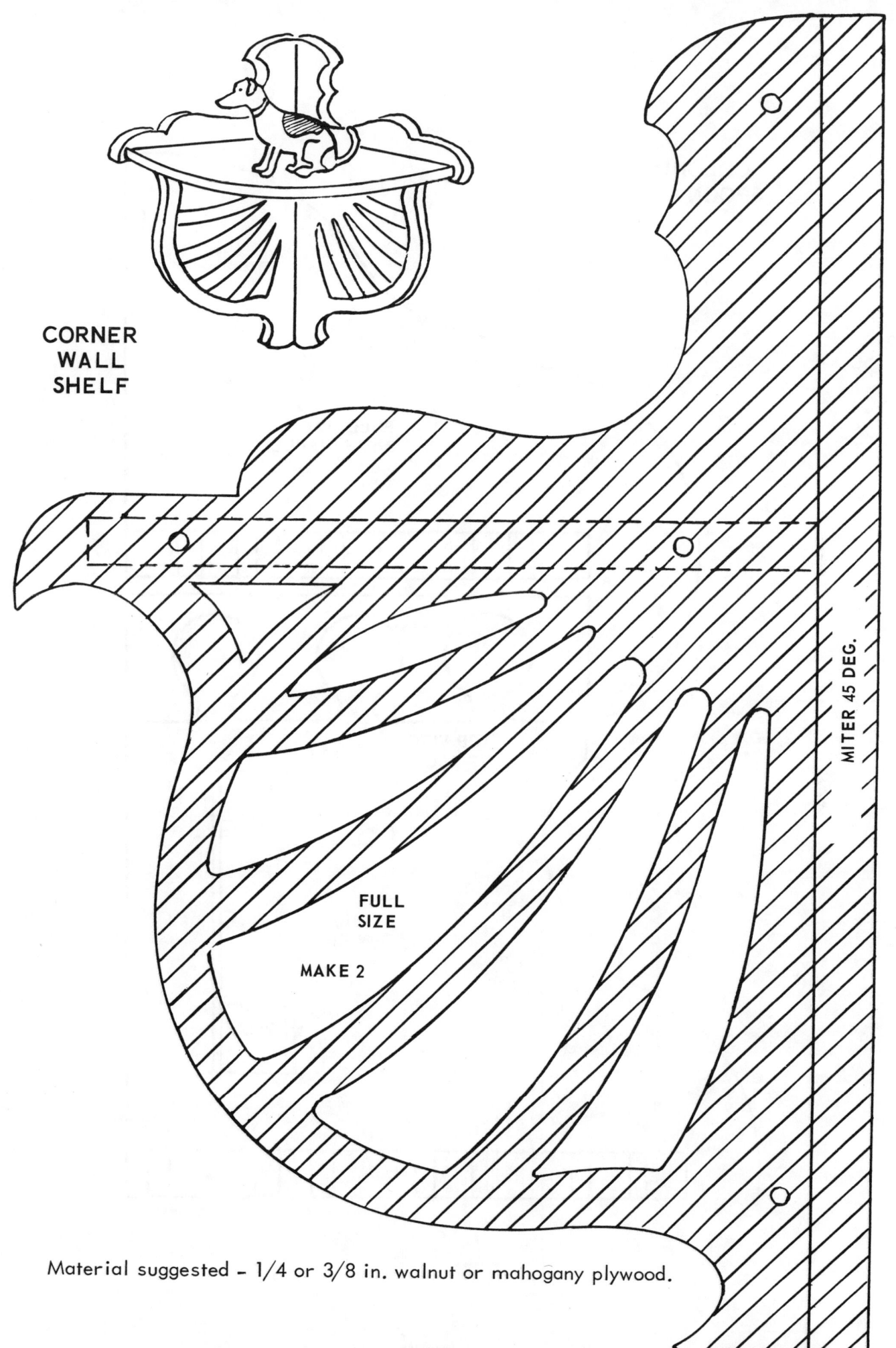

CORNER WALL SHELF

FULL SIZE
MAKE 2

MITER 45 DEG.

Material suggested – 1/4 or 3/8 in. walnut or mahogany plywood.

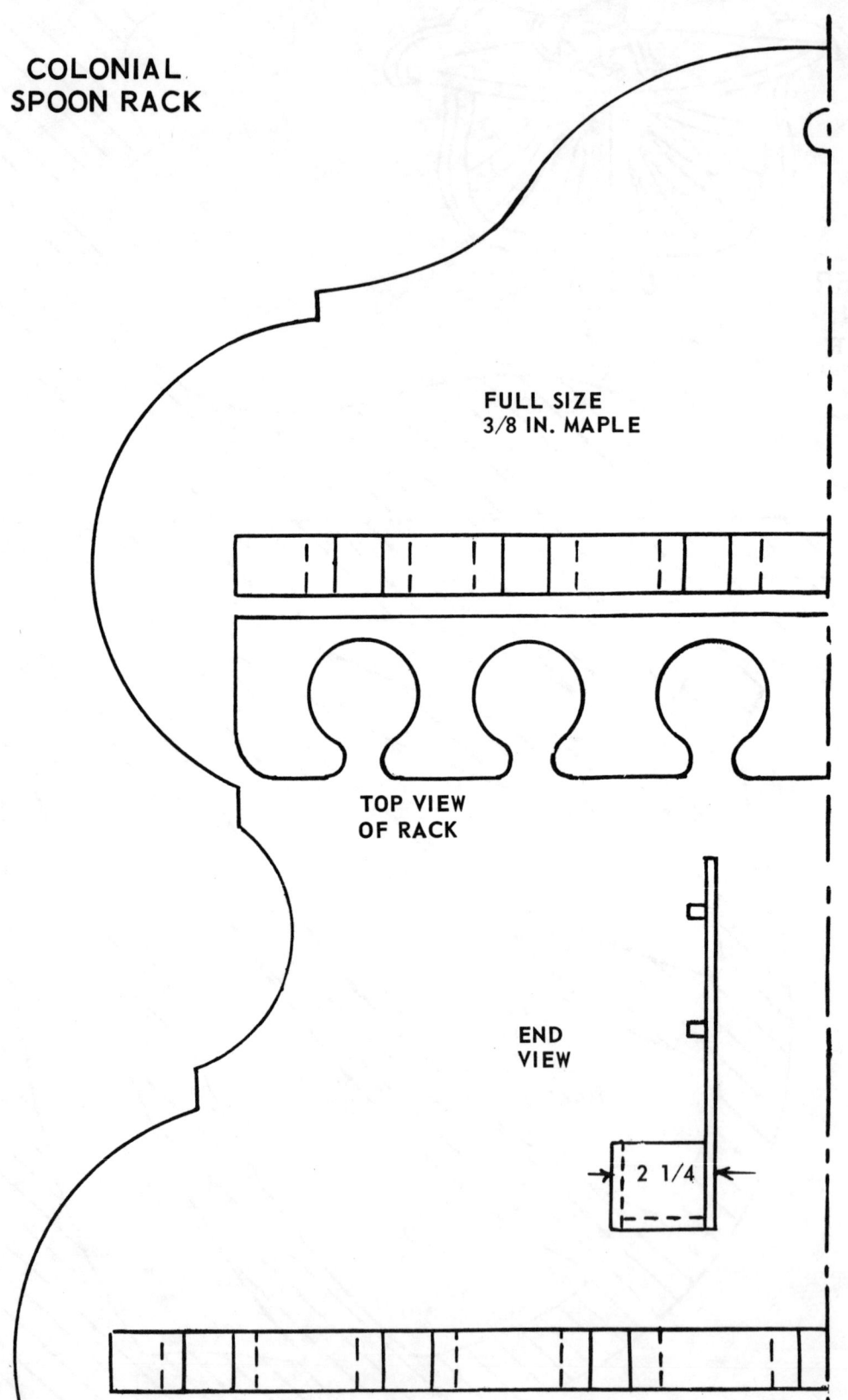

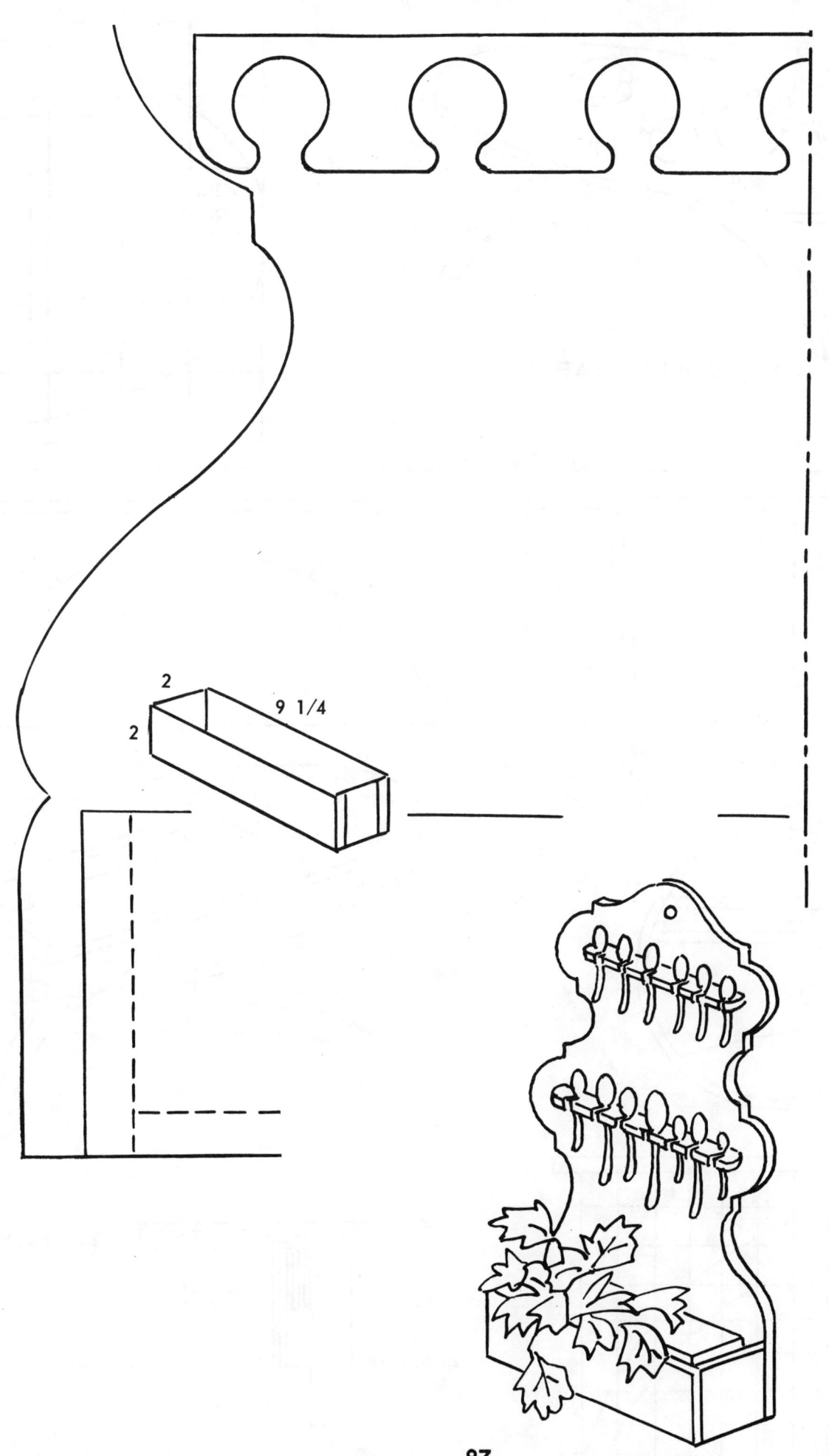

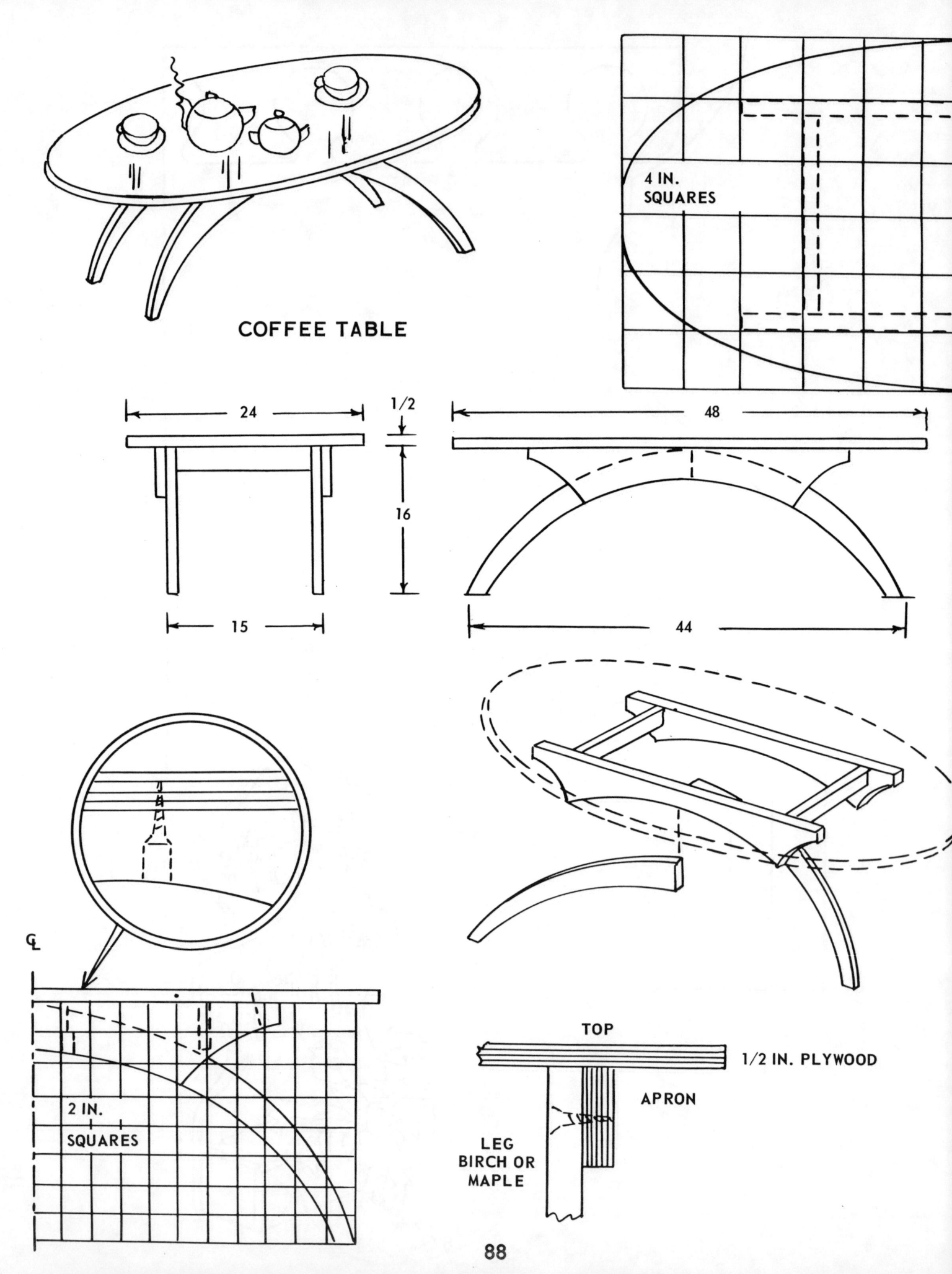

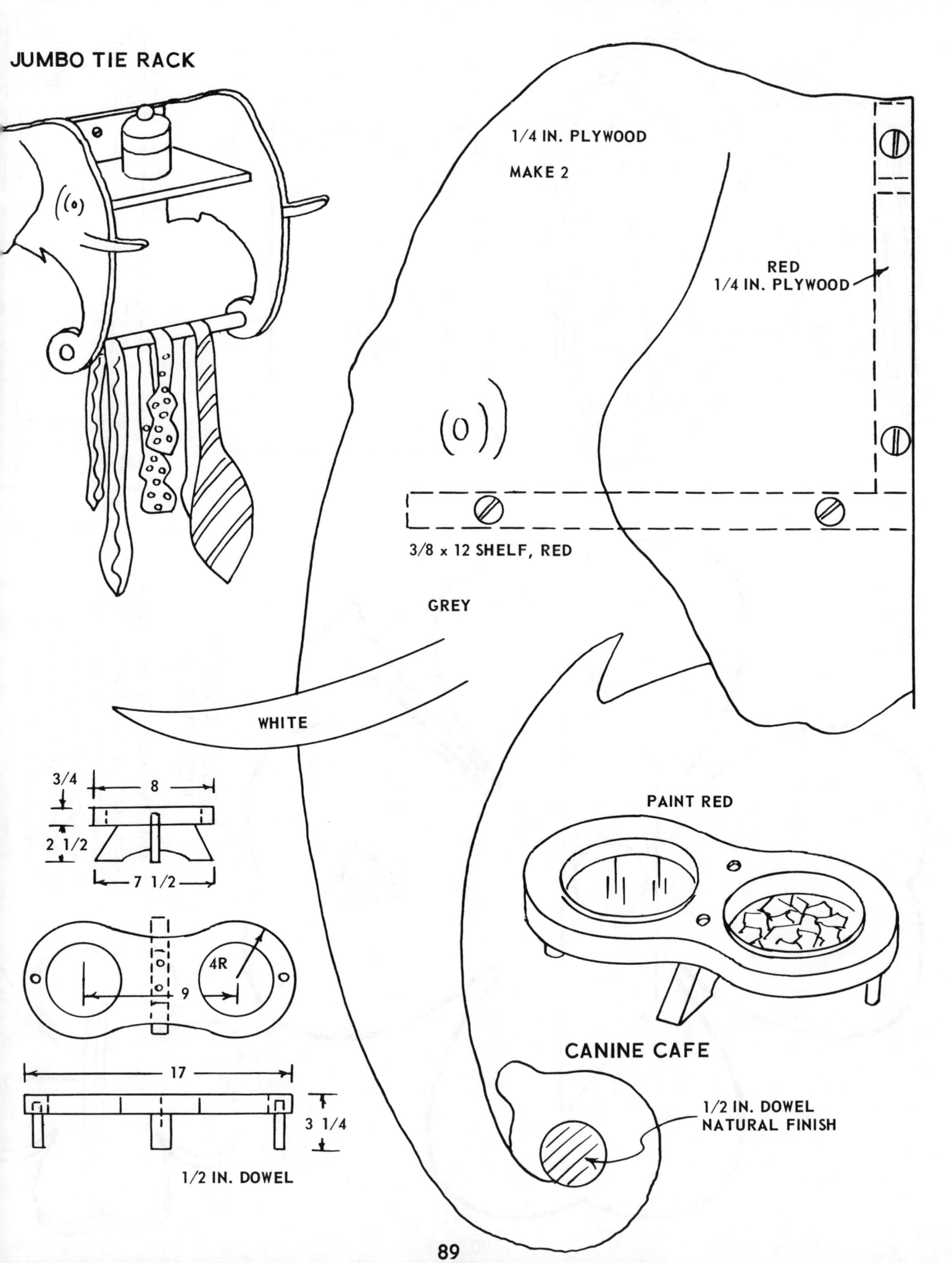

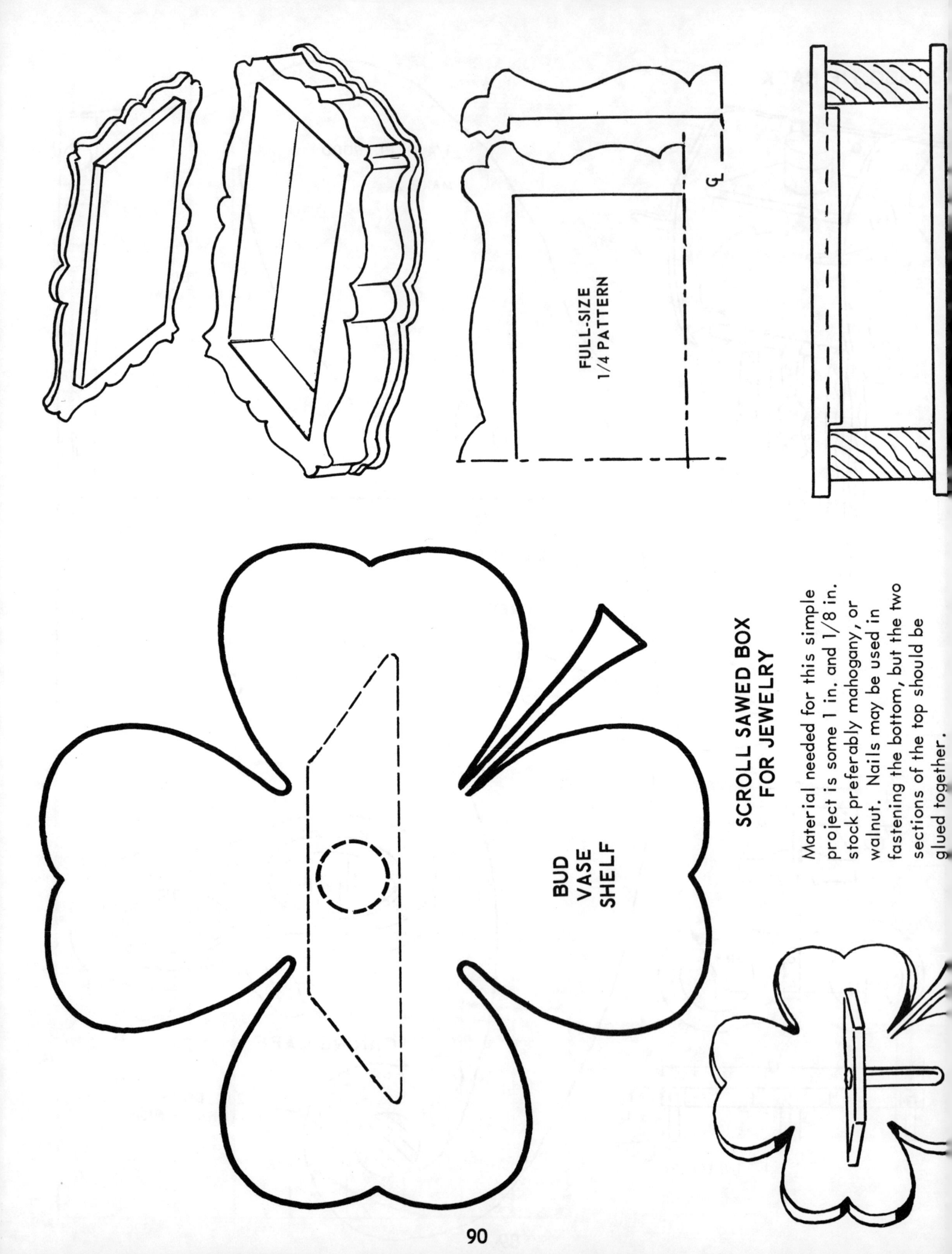

SCROLL SAWED BOX FOR JEWELRY

Material needed for this simple project is some 1 in. and 1/8 in. stock preferably mahogany, or walnut. Nails may be used in fastening the bottom, but the two sections of the top should be glued together.

BUD VASE SHELF

FULL-SIZE 1/4 PATTERN

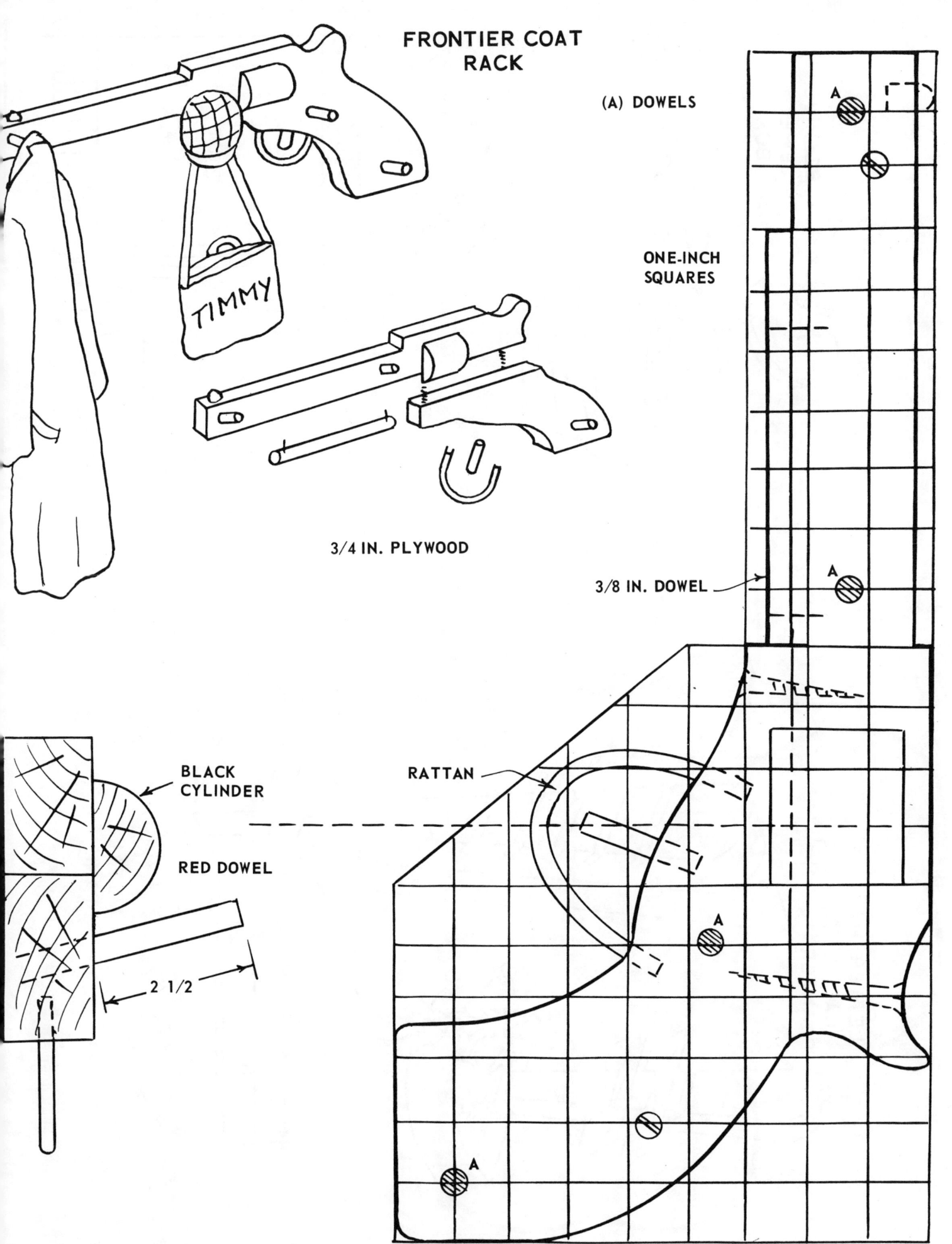

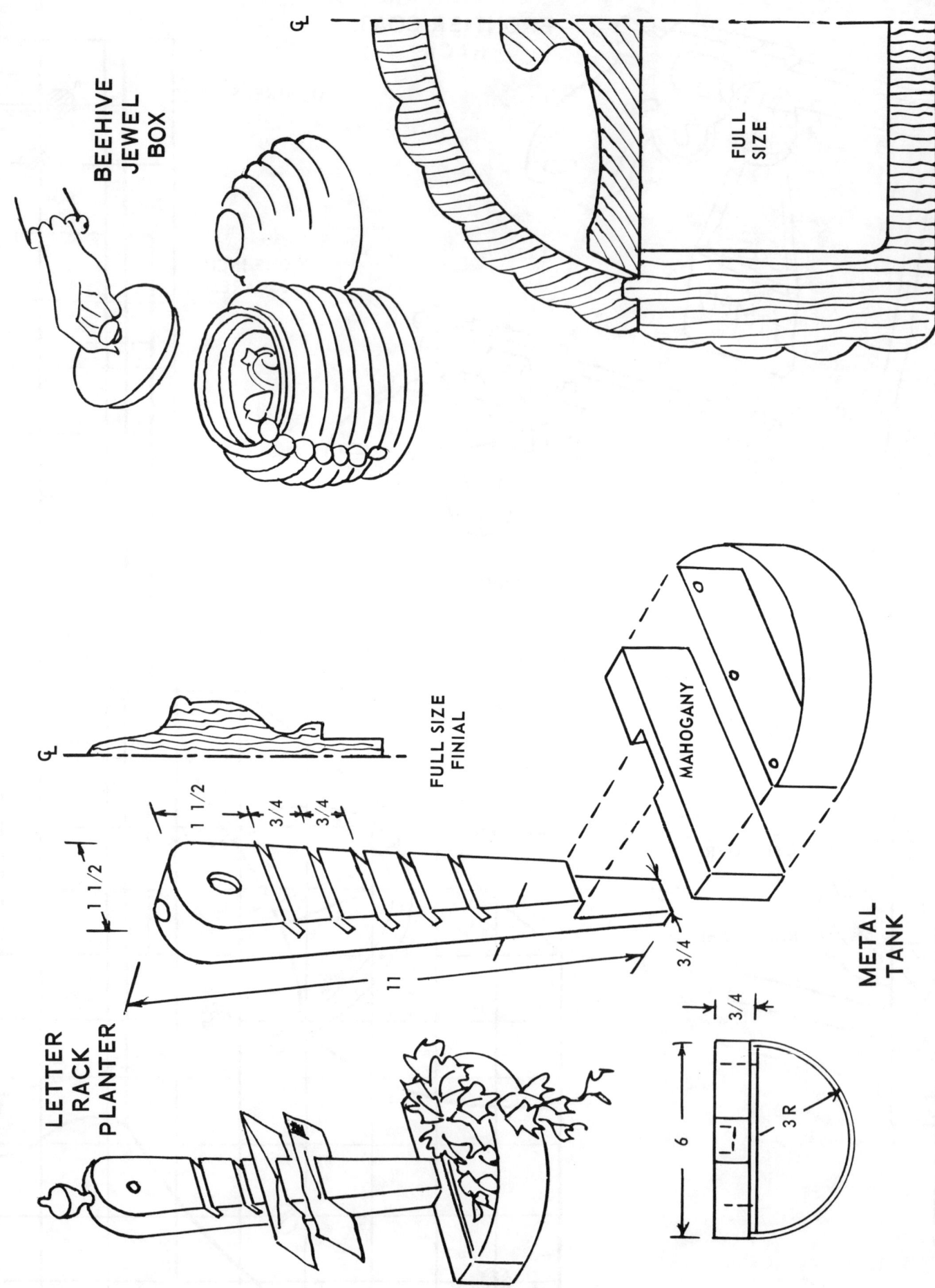

GOOD LUCK TIE RACK

KEY RACK

CLAMP HORSESHOE NAIL IN VISE AFTER DRIVING IT THROUGH 1/4 IN. PLYWOOD AND CLINCH

BRASS HOOKS FOR KEYS

FULL SIZE CALK

1/2 INCH SQUARES

FULL SIZE HALF PATTERN

1/4 IN. PLYWOOD

NAIL LOCATIONS

SAME SIZE AS AT RIGHT

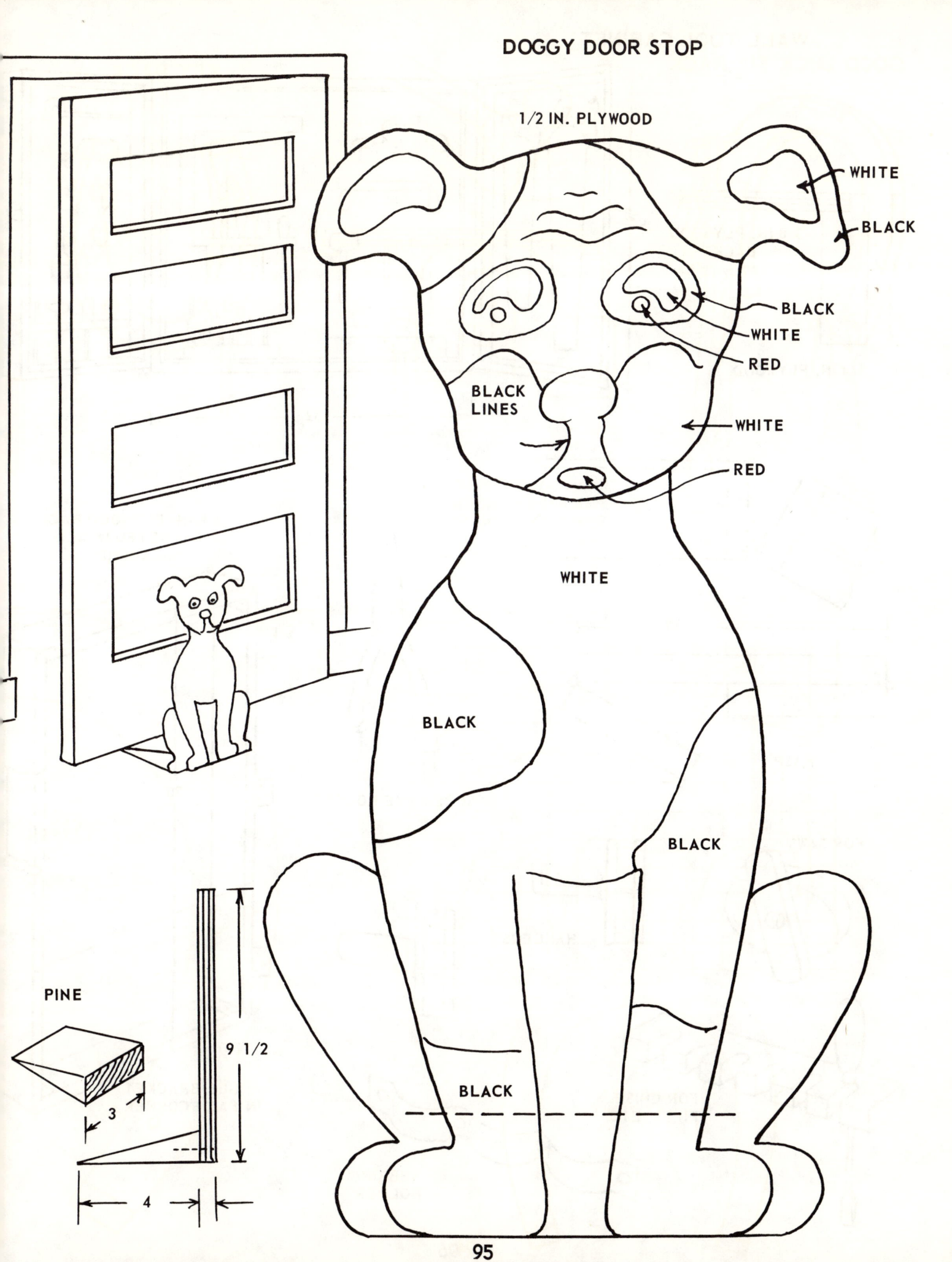

DOGGY DOOR STOP

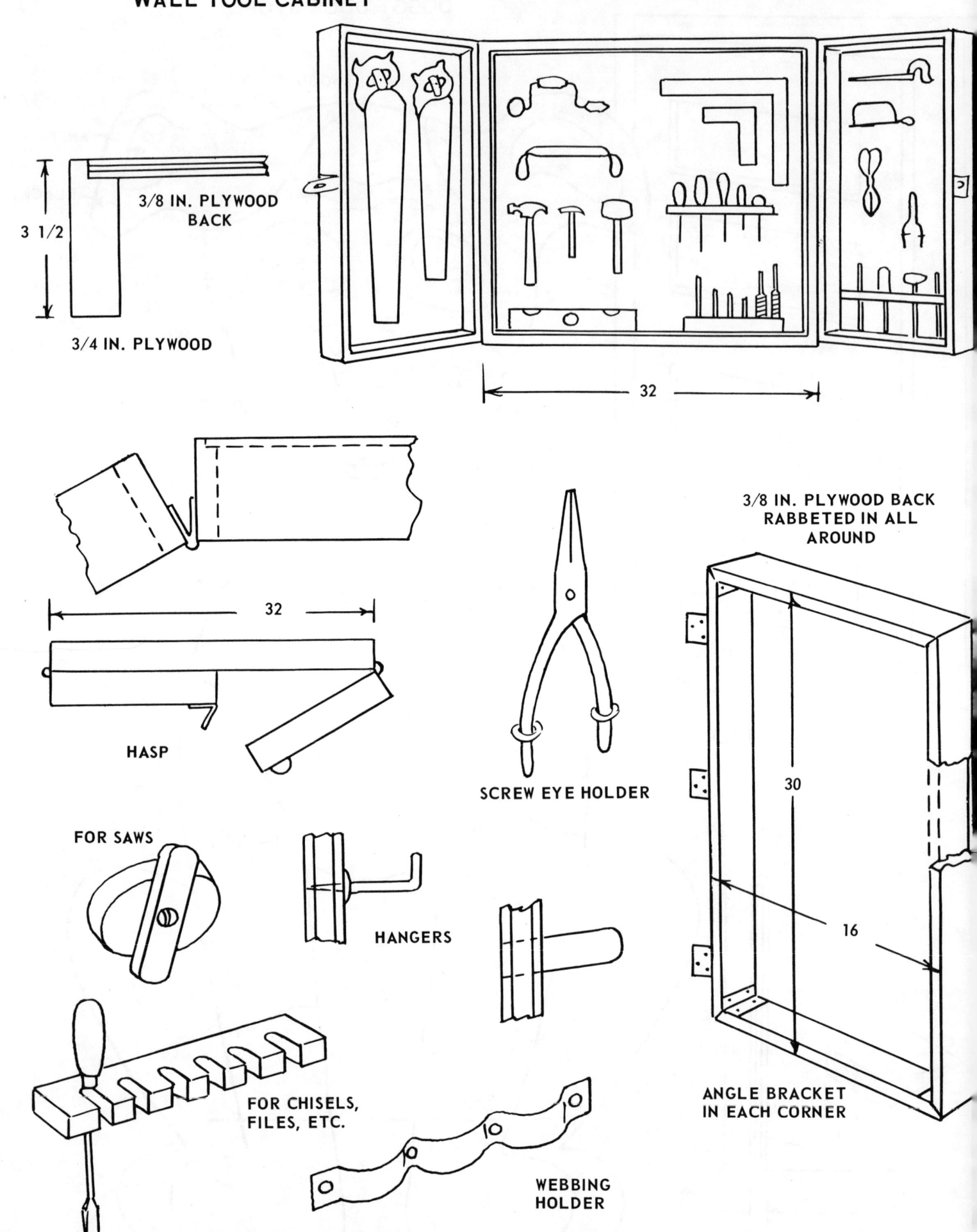